Fellowship Of The Dust

*On the High-line for Jesus—Because
Nothing Else Matters but God*

Jasmine Gregory

XULON PRESS

Kelly,
God Bless you,
Love 'n Christ
Jasmine

Fellowship of The Dust...

Xulon Press
2301 Lucien Way #415
Maitland, FL 32751
407.339.4217
www.xulonpress.com

© 2020 by Jasmine Gregory

All rights reserved solely by the author. The author guarantees all contents are original and do not infringe upon the legal rights of any other person or work. No part of this book may be reproduced in any form without the permission of the author. The views expressed in this book are not necessarily those of the publisher.

Unless otherwise indicated, Scripture quotations taken from the King James Version (KJV) – *public domain*.

Scripture quotations taken from the Holy Bible, New International Version (NIV). Copyright © 1973, 1978, 1984, 2011 by Biblica, Inc.™ Used by permission. All rights reserved.

Printed in the United States of America.

Paperback ISBN-13: 978-1-6322-1777-6

Contents

Introduction – On the Highline for Jesus.	vii
Chapter 1 – My Rose.	1
Chapter 2 – And so I Contemplate My Plight.	5
Chapter 3 – Scum of the Earth/Disguise Complete.	9
Chapter 4 – Fellowship of the Dust.	12
Chapter 5 – Backdoor Shopping.	17
Chapter 6 – Serving God – Inside out.	20
Chapter 7 – Finding the Gems.	24
Chapter 8 – Meekness isn't Weakness.	27
Chapter 9 – Taking Your Time; Ready – Set – Go! Hobo Talent Unveiled.	29
Chapter 10 – The Broken-Hearted.	32
Chapter 11 – Solace.	35
Chapter 12 – Outward Appearance.	36
Chapter 13 – Life is Not a Game of Chance.	39
Chapter 14 – Faith.	41
Chapter 15 – Not Act Holy—Be Holy.	44
Chapter 16 – Love Lifted Me.	46
Chapter 17 – Time.	49
Chapter 18 – Plumbline.	52
Chapter 19 – Death.	54
Chapter 20 – The First Time John Died.	57
Chapter 21 – The Healing Journey.	63
Chapter 22 – Airbags-Fears.	65
Chapter 23 – A Miracle in Indiana.	70
Chapter 24 – Turn Around.	73
Chapter 25 – Judgment Begins at the House of God.	77
Chapter 26 – The Blinding Power of God.	81
Chapter 27 – All of God's Creatures Shall Praise Him! – Revelations 5:13, Job 12:6-9.	87
Chapter 28 – Divine Intervention.	93

Chapter 29 – Big Foot! – Ephesians 6
"We fight not against flesh and blood....". 95
Chapter 30 – More Occult Encounters with Wicked Spirits in
High Places. 98
Chapter 31 – Testimony of a Drunken Man Set Free. 101
Chapter 32 – Language Barrier. 103
Chapter 33 – Hostility Diffused by the Holy Spirit. 105
Chapter 34 – A String of Pearls. 107
Chapter 35 – Heavenly Success. 109
Chapter 36 – Binding the Strong Man. 113
Chapter 37 – Boxcar Episodes. 116
Chapter 38 – Slice of Our Life – The Life of Riley. 120
Chapter 39 – Animal Encounters... A "Bear" Messenger. 122
Chapter 40 – Divine and Angelic Heavenly-Winged
Intervention. 125
Chapter 41 – No Bull – Macho! A Test. 128
Chapter 42 – Divine Appointments! – Malachi 3:16-18. 129
Chapter 43 – James Bond/Conspiracy-Treachery. 134
Chapter 44 – Battling the Storms in Weather and in People. 140
Chapter 45 – Gino: Eyes of Death. 145
Chapter 46 – On Women – Body Language. 149
Chapter 47 – Grey Ghost. 156
Chapter 48 – On Fire. 157
Chapter 49 – Klamath Falls – Jerry Encounter. 158
Chapter 50 – My "Original" Husband. 159

Introduction

– On the Highline for Jesus-because Nothing Else Matters but God

"For I think that God has set forth us apostles last as it were appointed to death: for we are made a spectacle unto the world, and to angels and to men. We are fools for Christ's sake, but ye are wise in Christ; we are weak, but ye are strong; ye are honorable, but we are despised. Even unto this present hour we both hunger, and thirst, and are naked, and are buffeted, and have no certain dwelling place; and labor, working with our own hands, being reviled we bless; being persecuted we suffer it. Being defamed, we entreat: we are made as the filth of the world and are the off scouring of all things unto this day." 1 Corinthians 4:9-13 KJV

The High-line is symbolic of giving up all for Christ— ready to be out in the field without income – trusting in Jesus – no certain dwelling place. To the world we were on the Low-line, the scum of the earth, but to God we were on the High-line to Heaven – the Call to Perfection – giving up all for Christ.

And boy does it transform you into that new Creature, a new Creation! The more people look at you as an "animal", or undisciplined children, "just kids" – the more you shine with the glory of God.

Actually, in freight train language, the High-line is just a route term. As we rode the Low-line plenty of times, for example, in Montana, the High-line is referring to the route from Spokane, Washington to Sandy Point, Idaho to White Fish, Montana to Havre, Montana into eventually Anoka, Minnesota – what a ride! Next if you take the Low-line in

Montana it's more southern and it goes through Spokane, Washington as well and Sandy Point, Idaho and then down to Missoula, Montana and Helena, Montana and Laurel, Montana.

It's like the Scottish say "you take the high road and I'll take the low road." Well there's nothing wrong with the low road, but to this day people use the metaphor for the right moral choice, for instance "take the high road and don't retaliate!"

So I am using the metaphor; "High-line" since we were freight train riders and after all, the High-line went through Glacier National Park and riding a piggy-back through there at night in the winter time with snow sparkling, cruising through the mountains it was just a little Heaven on earth! After all, gasp, but cold! And of course our Calling in Christ Jesus riding the freight trains was the High-line.

So now that we understand each other I can go on. My husband John was introduced to me as an "apostle" passing through at a Pentecostal church in California when I met him. So he is the "apostle John", of course, we didn't go around calling him that because me and John just weren't into titles – like our friends, the Friends (Quakers) are not. Apostle just means "sent one" – like a missionary.

Anyway, suffice it to say, you get out there in the hurly burly of lowly freight train riding or hitch-hiking life and you become the scum of the earth. So we embrace our title of "Nobodies for Jesus, who serve a great Somebody." Or "Schnooks for Jesus" – as that's the way everyone treated you, like you were a "schnook". But we knew we weren't schnooks, because we made the most intelligent wisest choice in the whole universe to give up all and follow the Pearl of Great Price, the Living Resurrected Savior, our Lord Jesus Christ! But to the world we were looked upon as schnooks, Fools for Christ – and believe me we had to get used to it. So John and I would call each other "schnooks" or "schnookie" sometimes as a favor, or reminder that we, like the apostle Paul would be misunderstood often. We even had a song, "Schnookie, oh so true, I love youuuuu!" And John would always do a little dance to cheer me up, when he sang it to me.

Yes, he was my darling, and I was his – my darling for life and I am a celibate now, after he died last year and graduated to glory, on May 22, 2006, his birthday. After 28 years of wedded bliss with my schnookie-pie lamb. (Who by the way traveled 36 years for Jesus with an ileostomy, yet, i.e. no large intestine and a bag on his side front)

Traveling the highways and byways and railroad tracks for Jesus our King! King of Kings and Lord of Glory!

Chapter 1

MY ROSE

Losing my husband John was like being hit by a freight train! Twenty-eight years of sublime Oneness erased in an instant. Our Oneness was in Christ even more enriching and our hearts were knit by the Cross of the Lord Jesus Christ that drew us together – I, at twenty-three years old, searching for my life's Calling – and being peculiarly drawn to a vagabond road-life, via backpack and all but wondering where to start. My husband already at it for seven years – full of testimonies and faith – meeting <u>me</u>, at twenty-three years old – he was thirty-seven almost thirty-eight, we became friends, best friends. And the Lord Jesus' cords of love drew us in a united plight and Calling to the mobile poor – the hitch hikers, the walkers, and later for twelve years more, the freight train riders. What a blessed experience of hair raising, gut-wrenching thrills and chills it was to be – and how well we learned to get along 24 hours a day and in often arduous challenges. No certain dwelling place – lack of food – lack of money – but blessed all the way because we were following the Lord Jesus our Lord and King! – our Savior and a Jealous God who watched over us with tender loving care. Keep in sight we were never "at ease" or "comfortable" but we were indeed under the Mighty hand of God, and what better Refuge is there–I can tell you–None Better!

Pleasant though it was, to live for Jesus in good 'ol USA, where vagabonds are still allowed though – frowned upon – but nonetheless not entirely <u>outlawed</u>. It's our freedom! As in other lands that have dictators and are militant, the bum or tramp is outlawed, and no such person exists. Oh the "avant garde" or "bourgeois" person might laugh now and say, "<u>good</u>" but really, this <u>is</u> the ultimate freedom , to be able to, without being monitored, to know that you can do that, take off if you have to or want to; true euphoria in a callous culture of democratic contradictions – So much for true blue American pie – we landed into a sub-culture of hippies, wandering veterans, travelers of all ethnic backgrounds and ages, some of ill-repute and full of earthy wisdom and diverse talents.

Getting back to the rad–radical life of our homeless Calling we were entirely living and <u>alive</u> in such an existence – Not at all religious but God-fearing; not at all uptight but holy – not at all needy though scarce – not at all greedy though freely giving – bent on the One, the prize of the High Calling – the Son of the most high God – the Lover of all mankind – Jesus our Lord and King, who died on the Cross for our sins and rose again on the third day – and His calling – a Vagabond – a despicable disguise for the righteous King of Kings – to get His message out in a most enticing, but unconventional way! Power in humility and <u>so we found out</u>!

Dense though the bourgeoisie society was to such illicit freedoms, we were <u>Kings of the Road</u>, serving a most amazing King, who did the same thing, and so encouraged us, for He was with us in a mighty way. He was our shield and buckler, and our rod and our staff.

How? When we slept we prayed for His protection, when we moved we prayed for His protection – where we went, how we went, where we slept – we prayed for His direction. The choice was His whether we hitch-hiked, just walked, or rode a freight train – the journey was mapped out by God Almighty on the highways and byways, and railroad tracks to find those lost souls, those heartbroken souls – those "divine appointments," that need direction and restoration, to be set free! And we would find them under bridges, beside fires, by the railroad tracks, right on the freight trains and sometimes inside cars when we put our thumb out. It was a hard task, but one we could never do on our own – We were led by an invisible Hand – by an invisible God.

It was <u>not</u> us, it was Him… our hands, our eyes, our lives, were not our own – but His! And so we mystically found the <u>just right fruit</u>, ready to be picked for God. How supernatural! And... it was not us, it was Him – we did not strive or cry out in streets – it was Christ in us Living, and Moving and Being through us, to find just the right person, at just the right time, with unfathomable depth in our despicable disguise – with no secret bank accounts to back us up or church organizations to back us up, Only Jesus Our Rock – the Richness of God, working with the emptiness of man in a most creative way, in remote places. Well, I can only compare this all to my most unprofitable days as a sinner when I searched for God – throughout high school and college, seeking His real face – and finding only confusion and other religions and diverse gods until one day I ran into a brick wall in my endless search. With an older friend of eight years, we decided to search all night for God in 1976 with any book we could find like Confucius, Buddha, you name it, and at 3 o'clock in the morning my friend and I found her aunt's Bible so we decided to check it out. I woke up with a thunder bolt as I spontaneously read John 14:6 to her, Jesus said "I am the way, the truth and the life, no man cometh to the Father but by me." And I realized He indeed was the zenith of them all who did not proclaim to be a mere teacher to "guide" us to a path or light, but indeed was the "Light", "the Way, and the Truth and Life" itself – And so I knew from that day forward, at 21 years old, as did my friend, that much like those lost or stumbled souls I would meet on the railroad – that God met us in a mystical way, when we searched for Him with all our heart – He found us out!

Happy days are here again, the skies are blue, we have a Friend, and light is shining through me from Him, to you!

The Rose is a Rose and he Arose!
He arose in my life, a man,
A man who said, "I can."
A man who was a Rose to me –
I saw him across the room
and he motioned to me –
I arose to go to him
and he conversed with me,
about the Lord Jesus Christ...

I knew him to be my true love
(And by and by)
I gave my rose (my virtue to him)
He was a rose to me – a friend!
The "Rose of Sharon," brought us together—
The Lord Jesus Christ, King of Kings, and Lord of Lords.
For 28 years my rose dwelt with me—we paid the price,
and we were free, and we walked, hitch-hiked,
and we rode the freight trains –
all for the glory of the Lord Jesus Christ!
We lived an arduous, rough life, and lived in blissful harmony—
and he, my amorous spouse, was always a Rose to me...
One sad early morning after prolonged illness –
on his 66th birthday — the enemy slayed him.
He arose suddenly and fell in my arms and he died after 28 years.
And I cried – for his spirit left him.
I took "my Rose," <u>my</u> virtue, back again –
As his spirit rose to meet Jesus,
Our Friend in the Heavenlies –
Time marched on...
And I tossed and I turned
with my rose virtue in tact –
yearning to be with him, my prince, a king in the end, my prize John.
So I took my rose (my virtue)
and I flung it back to the Lord Jesus my King of Kings –
the Rose of Sharon, My Eternal Prize! –
To be His celibate prize, His Bride! ... Unless He leads otherwise!
And so I made peace with my terrible loss –
and knowing my John was irreplaceable to me!
I arose, a celibate to serve my King, and Savior, Lord Jesus,
who died and rose again for me!
<u>He</u> is my Rose, forever, Now!
And He doth say, "I can" Hallelujah!
For Our Savior, who died and rose again!
That we might live through Him.

Chapter 2

AND SO I CONTEMPLATE MY PLIGHT

So here I am hidden in my tent by the railroad tracks, a widow now – accepting the loss of my husband, my hero! Alone – but still at peace with my Lord Jesus Christ and the birds and other creatures, though missing my beloved after only 13 months. I did after all, agree to suffer the loss of all things – for the perfect knowledge of Jesus Christ – Just didn't think it meant my beautiful husband.

Of course, with life on the road Life is perilous and we often face death – So I really did face his loss so many times and John would always say, "Remember, dear Jasmine, I am on loan-lease to you and you're on loan-lease to me." But the inebriating high of seeing God's, Holy Spirit and His Angels, deliver you so many times from such dangers and perilous people, it does start to make one feel bullet proof after awhile! There is a thin line between arrogance and faith – and it is so important to know when you're crossing it… And so that's another "whole topic".

Back to the loss of my Faithful and Beloved friend – As I reflected on our travels – I found myself realizing the inexplicable sovereignty of God – and came to the determined reality of surrendering this loss, after all – My life is not my own – my husband was on loan-lease, as he said. And even in his later years, if the illness was due to treachery, perpetrators of evil, and liars – he was indeed well taken care of now and in an exquisitely "Better place", Heaven!

So, I relaxed a bit more and the blues became more of a jubilation, and "rejoicing to be exceedingly glad for great is our reward in Heaven – for so persecuted they the prophets before you!"

And so I know that my saintly John – was exceedingly greatly rewarded in Heaven, as a much persecuted prophet, and a humble servant of the Lord Jesus Christ. And so I tried to leap a little but my backpack was too heavy with groceries and water. "Later" I said! Because it <u>does</u> say "leap for joy" if you read the beatitudes. So it was a Great reward indeed! And I breathed a sigh of relief... As Deceit is one of the worst enemies to meet in souls when you are open and sincere.

Next Home?
What shall my next house be like?
Oh, What shall it be like? –
This one is so exquisite...
Two side windows, a welcome mat – a tall back window
A peaking Roof that rises like a "dome"—
A pleasant pale green and teal green interior
An exterior sheen of minty and teal green!
Oh how Serene!
There are awnings too, to shield me from the rain
—And a sumptuous floor to exercise upon.
It is divided neatly by me – a bathroom corner,
A mat for my bed – clothes in back – and sandals in front
—With my Bible and other important things.
The birds tweet merrily beside me
flitting about, through my large circular door I view them.
—And! My husband laid here!
It was our last home – you see – a three man tent!
I wonder will I be able to let it go...
My mate for life lay down here – and we were One for 28 years.
—My soul-mate, we seldom had strife –
I was his wife for life, and he was my other half,
faithful and true—we loved each other to the end –
So what shall I do?
The zippers broke – And so am I –

And So I Contemplate My Plight

And once the door goes... oh my...
It's at least 4 years old and that's pretty good –
As we used it every day – as we lived this way.
Camping outdoors in God's great glory—
Being in the pines, the walnut groves, the Aspens,
and sometimes having a little stove
It was fine as we rode the freight trains—
Oh so sublime –
What a rigorous, lovely life –
All for the Lord Jesus Christ
And I was his missionary wife,
My beloved John and I.
But now I am alone – Alone with Our God –
Our God who protected us through storms and adventures
and perils...
Marauders, deceivers, and rapists, too –
We were never touched – by the virulent enemy
—Blessed – and trusting in God Almighty
Oh, what a blessed friend and fountain of life we have in the Lord
Jesus Christ – our Covering.
The hardest one though was treachery
— Though it wasn't always hard to see
Other times it took our breath away in subtlety
—And my husband died from the treacherous games people play –
a Champion, he was, but weakened by an ileostomy – 42 years.
He fought to the end – then losing his kidneys again from
treachery –
Then onward Christian soldier he went and then he was spent –
The enemy moved in to target him again...
But he sailed off in Victory – to a Heavenly Realm – leaving me
with our tent – a broken zipper now – and a sleeping bag I hug
at night –
wishing my sweet husband would hold me tight
as I shiver through the cold starry night...
But then – I have my God, my Great Friend,
who always held me in His Hand – the Holy Ghost – comforts me –
He's always with me and Lord Jesus gives me His bread of Life

as I meditate on His great sacrifice
The Father in Heaven gives me Fatherly love, lavishing me in tender care
— And so I don't entirely despair—
Still missing my beloved husband friend, of 28 years, so very much ...
And the Angels protect me in the night as the animals surround me in furry delight,
raccoons and possums...
And so I contemplate my plight! Good night!

Chapter 3

SCUM OF THE EARTH/DISGUISE COMPLETE

"A rich man is wise in his own conceit but the poor man who has understanding searches him out." If you have experienced the other side of the coin – poverty – you will know this well. I got to experience both. I grew up in middle class existence; house, family, two cars, college graduate, my dad an accountant of a big company, etc. Next... at 23 ½ years old – after a born again revival of my soul (at almost 22 yrs. old), I gave up all to follow Jesus and <u>gained</u> a husband, and lost my family I grew up with. I became of no reputation and gained the <u>best</u> husband in the world. Soon I discovered the other side of the coin, that people love you for "status" and "money". It is absolutely true that a drug dealer with bucks and a mansion will get more respect in society, than a humble respectable bum or transient. Why? Because they can flash those buckaroos and smile a wattage smile capped in gold teeth. No wonder some poor trampled groups, who are marginalized in society, go that route. They finally get respect! But the end result, of course, is unbearable inward poverty... So even though I would flash my college graduate, former middle class smile – no one cared anymore! All they saw was my disheveled clothes, dirty face, backpack and lack of resources and oh we smelled they thought, at least to their elite noses, as we shared our cup of coffee in McDonalds... Well, to make a long story short, we were the "scum of the earth" – our disguise was complete! 1 Corinthians 4:10 "Fools for Christ."

So along this ragged road experience, you might think, I was just on a "trip" – having an off-beat good time... But it was really more serious than this. Think about this – our life on the road, which lasted nearly all of our 28 years, give or take a few year breaks, with one year off in an apartment and a few years in people's homes, but most of the time in the great outdoors. Even when my husband was sick and on dialysis we remained outdoors, except that last year and a half, of the 4 ½ years he was on dialysis. And then, when he was 66 year old, on his birthday he died – Quite a Birthday – present. He graduated to Glory.

Anyway – we were quite happy outside, while he could still make it, because we were so acclimated to it, after years of traipsing it all over the USA… even Hawaii. Being a bum, or the correct word really is "tramp" – for the Lord Jesus. The old time word was "hobos" – but now they call themselves, "tramps," instead of "hobos" – that ride the freight trains – and are <u>glad</u> to say they are tramps! But of course, if a bourgeois person calls them that, it is always an insult. So we said we were tramps for the Lord Jesus Christ, unashamedly, though an ambiguous term for a women by myself, because it could insinuate whoredom. And I was faithful to my husband all 28 years, and now I'm a single celibate so I think I'll have to switch to, "gypsy for Jesus," lest I give the wrong impression. We became champions of the road-life in our faith, and that's why my beloved could even take his downhill years of deteriorating health, my John "Ariel" (Lion of God) spent, and spent, for the Kingdom of God.

And so now I am a recluse—a female monk, seeking only His approval – after healing in a shelter with many people for 10 months, after the shock of losing my mate, then I went outside again, to discern, the voices of society trying to dictate to me what my Calling must become without my beloved, my banquet of love by my side – a resolute, down to earth, humble man, of a deeply spiritual life that poured right out of his pores – an anointing of a sold-out missionary, with the mystery of godliness in him.

He was a candle to me and I became one too, but he taught me so much from his own pioneer wandering of 7 years, and 9 years of a holy life, and as an older man – having much wisdom – 14 ½ years my senior. And he was actually saved at the tender age of 12 years old, and filled with the Holy Ghost at a Kathryn Kuhlman revival – the great evangelist, who through the power of God wrought many authentic miracles.

She often came to Carnegie hall in Pittsburg, Pennsylvania, and at 12 years old with ulcerative colitis, he stood up to receive Jesus and got knocked down by the power of God and spoke in other tongues as a Catholic boy, who knew nothing of such things in 1952.

And with that background check, I will carry on to the ever-exciting adventures of two humble, lowly travelers who gave up all to be in the Life of Jesus.

Anyway, I am what I am – And that is <u>not</u> socially acceptable – it was so easy to take, with a mate-for-life, (the onslaughts of the enemy), but by myself, I ponder – can I...? Well, so far okay, but I'm just new at this after a year of being outdoors alone. And I am finding that the same Presence of the Lord that was with me and John, still abides here and protects me mightily – the Lord Jesus Christ, and the Holy Spirit, and the Father in Heaven, and His-ever-present Angels!

Chapter 4
Fellowship of the Dust

In the first 10 months alone, Jesus built up my faith, so that I could live with a whole hodge-podge of people in a shelter when I couldn't handle life alone, and was comforted by people. Then when he released me from there, He, the Lord Jesus, gave me solace and showed me I could camp alone "gorilla style" just as I always had done with my husband, and as always, the Lord Jesus' presence comforted me even alone, by the railroad tracks, in an abandoned orchard. Though I had a husband full of faith and fruits of the Holy Spirit, it was again the Lord Jesus in my husband and in myself that made me feel so sublime!

We were, after all, sometimes under filthy bridges with excrement and cobwebs, waiting on Jesus for one soul—for three days in Bakersfield, CA or another time in Portland, OR finding those gems, those lost gold coins Jesus was after. One man coughing up blood under a bridge from too much alcohol—us talking to them until they were able to tell us their spiritual needs and off we take them on the freights with us, up to Seattle, WA to the detox center they liked. Now they were ready, after being patched up for three days, with prayer, fellowship, and hope in God. This was our exciting life with the devastatingly deep love of God… searching the unsearchable—souls that hid out in the "unwanted" zones—hoping to find peace of mind… A lot of these men are veterans from wars of awful memories—Vietnam, Korea, and even those from WWII were out there still roughing it for 20 years, quite the champions of the road and really brave, despite bad habits, in some cases, they were overcoming. These men were overcoming a slew of things—to be free… with herculean strength, against the current of society.

We live in a free society—but you soon find out when you're "out there"—how much the antichrist rules in subtle ways to break men down—to conform <u>before</u> they are healed—to perform –to follow the rules—it's a formula for disaster if they don't realize their need to be transformed and healed first. And to find their own solution and peace of mind in one of those ways, is to take off and to get out of the box and travel low style, and rethink your history, your value system, and face God with the bare essentials. And so we did, and so they did! The cruelties of war are soon soothed and anesthetized by the realities of an adventurous, on the edge existence—much like they experienced in Vietnam minus some of the terrorizing after effects, although you do meet your share of rough men out there who are predatory.

I saw the soldierly existence is far closer to reality and the real world—in a microcosm though, of intense conflict and death! –then the romantic dream world of the middle class society… So just imagine the soldier who went through four years of straits returning to the white picket fence dream-world of TV, and watching ballgames, and 8 to 5 jobs. And you have men, after having witnessed death and having killed, who <u>need</u> a reason to live!

So live they did in high gear—railroad riding, freewheeling life, as humble as pie, existence—but at last, a chance to be alive… Yes, they let men tell them in their teenage adulthood how to handle a gun, they let them tell them how to march, how to be united, how <u>not</u> to succumb to the enemy, how to retreat—And they let men tell them how to kill… A piece of their soul was taken for the real or unreal war—And they sure weren't going to let society tell them how to live after all that—no way—to return it as if it never happened, that supreme trial of facing death and watching others die—sometimes pulling the trigger and causing death before you're old enough to know the damage and toll it would take on your soul… Now to come back and act like nothing happened, nosiree. So they took off in a bundle of soldierly strength, and we met them and appreciated them, and lots of them knew Jesus already—and Jesus renewed them for their efforts to know the truth— and the truth set them free.

These men carved out an existence for themselves—picking fruit, doing odd jobs, picking cans, checking the dumpsters for free food like grocery stores, though a lot of good food was thrown away in fast food places for example. So it was all about survival... they built shacks in cold places like Bend, OR and enjoyed the challenge of the great outdoor life immensely!

That's the audience we had, the people we met. Once in a while, a few women, like "Boxcar Jan" (an ex-marine), and an American Indian women who said she had the great outdoors in her blood—but mostly men. We would meet these folks under bridges and they'd invite us to a cup of coffee brewed to hobo perfection—fresh grounds, and if you boil them in a pot or can the grounds will eventually clear out and you can pour it off—very simple... so good. And we'd thank them for their hospitality and talk about anything and everything—the latest dumpster finds, the glorious freight train rides, our personal histories and woes, and finally God would always come up like a huge balloon that can't be pushed into the water. God would always rise up—without us trying, proselytizing, or hinting—it was easy— This was fellowship! We called it the fellowship of the hobos or the fellowship of the dust. So these were broken men—who wore their sins on their sleeves—who knew how to travel—and be themselves.

The Fellowship of the Dust

My husband John was a broken man, with divine confidence, on the road for Jesus for seven years when I met him – And together we got more broken, first hitch-hiking, then more lowly freight train riding – having to lose our reputation, forget who we are and learn to be the essence of who you really are. So we started out a somebody – and you become a nobody. So we used to say, when folks said "who do you think you are?" – "We're nobodies who serve a great Somebody! God!"

This is true fellowship, breaking the bread of sincerity and truth, together, without all the pretense and masks – just yourself – And then lo and behold – as God is <u>near</u> to a broken heart – so He arrives – to bless this fellowship, under the bridge, where His name is spoken, <u>not</u> under compulsion – for service – but out of pure love! For all of us had seen the hand of God touch us from time to time – from the holy rollers like me and John – to the common sinners, with a mustard seed of faith – we'd all seen God save our necks when we called on Him, with <u>no</u> props to hold us up anymore – <u>not</u> fine suits, or bank accounts, or neighbors, or friends, or houses, or cars, but only the <u>living God who could save our necks out there in the absolute vulnerability of Road-Life existence</u> – And so we shared our stories of His Presence in our hazardous lives – with espresso coffee wake-ups – lives of survival in fringes of existence – And we all new well... God was alive! ...And a <u>very</u> present help in time of trouble.

Now you know why Paul the apostle commended Pricilla and Aquilla – apostle traveling couple – not for their theology or book-learning or even preaching – but because they "risked their neck for the Lord Jesus Christ!" Romans 16:3-4, NIV/KJV. Now you know why he said this – it's what proves your faith and brings you closer to God, face to face – to who He is! It brings you to a fine revelation! <u>Nothing</u> else <u>matters</u> <u>but</u> <u>God</u>!

So here I sit with my little bird friends thinking how much I matured and grew in such an atmosphere in lowly tent-dwelling, but true edge of reality existence – from my twenties to my thirties to my forties – I was fifty-one and a half when my husband died – he was sixty-six years old <u>on</u> <u>that</u> <u>very</u> <u>day</u> – though he looked forty-five! Despite his physical short-comings and sufferings. It <u>was</u> fun!

Me, at almost 49 yrs. old, near RR tracks. John took pic.

Chapter 5
BACKDOOR SHOPPING

How do you get inside someone's soul – how do you know what makes them tick – You can't! Only the Holy Ghost can really penetrate into someone's inner sanctum – Only He knows man's innermost thoughts...

So God used to press into their inner sanctums with amazing laser accuracy – and enable them to see where they were – heading to – and why – and what was good about their life – and it was truly mystical...

Now for the fun – What was fun about our ragged on the edge existence was the wonderful, child-like faith you got to see rewarded. One time I had a vision I found a dime in the restroom – I said to the Lord – should I pick it up? Well, this was prophetic – and for the next six weeks we lived on a dime and we didn't see a dollar or even have enough money for coffee. We found food in the dumpsters wherever we went, from Colton, California, to Klamath Falls, Oregon, to Seattle, Washington, to Spokane, Washington to Missoula, Montana and back and the Lord met our needs in simplicity with give-away clothes, and the old hobo-trick of finding "used grounds" from a restaurant and making weak coffee, by the side of the road – It was so rewarding to see you could live without money – not to be paralyzed by fear – to know God can take care of you in all kinds of conditions – and still keep you happy! We never starved – we never had regret – we were happy... It was as simple as that.

So you can imagine what I felt like when I came out of a middle-class lifestyle, and was suddenly on a twenty-five mile walk – with no food in sight until the next town – but somehow we survived – and in town we'd find a dumpster behind a grocery store filled with loaves of bread and blocks of cheese – a gift from Jesus. Or I remember walking into a big city and finding a whole lime pie thrown away. It was always possible to look behind fast food joints and find a pizza still in the box – or half of one uneaten – or a hamburger joint with hamburgers in boxes thrown away untouched because of the ten minute health law – because not enough customers came that time – or a donut place with a bag of untouched donuts, just the end of the day and out they go. And grocery stores with delis were great at the end of the day because they throw away little bags of cheese and meat all in one big bag, nice and clean.

> So we survived like the hobos riding the freight trains and we truly reveled in our freedoms in God's glory in hidden extremes and a humble disguise.
> Hallelujah, Hallelujah, Hallelujah!

When we checked the dumpsters we felt like big kids, finding the delightful prize – sometimes deli meats, roast beef, chicken, pastrami, cheese wrapped in plastic all wrapped up in a clean bag – bunches of canned good, candy bars, cakes! It was amazing how much food Americans throw away! It was surreptitious fun – and the irony of it was – people were often ridiculing us for our lowly, impoverished existence, and God was preparing a table for us, a banquet – in the presence of His enemies. We had no class – But what class God had – to leave an avenue of nourishment to those lowly mountain-high travelers. (As one brother in Christ said to us, I wonder where those ravens got the food to feed Elijah? God only knows!) Of course – all the lowly poor, saints and sinners alike, could be fed this way, if they were humble enough to dine in that dumpster and not care what others think. All it cost was our bourgeois pride. As John would always sing to me when we had a good find, and with a little dance, "Back-door shopping, back-door shopping, Compliments of the Holy Ghost, all it will cost us is our bourgeois pride!"

John and I had a great life together. Our life together – <u>It was beautiful</u>! Words can't describe how hidden was the power and the grace of God in our dusty clothes and faces – as we walked the hundreds of miles and traveled via freight train and thumbing it. We were wrapped in the mystery of God in our extreme humility and vulnerability – You are our hiding place Oh God – You surround us with songs of deliverance. "Jesus was our Rock in a weary land". Our shield and buckler from the wolves and foxes and coyotes out there – Not just the animals – but the ones in people – those we <u>really</u> needed protection from... No, this was no starry-eyed traveling, where you could just buy your "supposed" safety, and hide in exquisite suites. This was the rugged outdoors, penniless, traveling on a wing and a prayer – moving by the grace of God – with utter abandon to His will – living by faith. And not only that, it was romantic traveling all over with my true love – life in jeopardy – but yet, always safe in God's heavenly places.

To our families and bourgeois acquaintances we were reckless – but to Our God – we were safe. As long as we followed Him and traveled in His perfect will... His anointing protected and covered us. God was and is our Refuge... We carried our crosses (our backpacks) and followed Him... After a weary rest on a long walk – John would say, "we better get going and pick up our cross," and so we did and off we'd go, walking another 10 miles to the nearest town.

Why walk – because Jesus would tell us to walk. Some people will pick you up if they see you walking, or some people won't – But it was all according to <u>God's</u> plan. Walking was a catharsis for us – a time to be cleansed – until we met the next soul. And sometimes we'd be walking and God would chasten one of us with a sharp pain. It felt like a cattle prod, an electric current in my back. I'd say, "John, I'm getting chastened." He'd nod, "I know Jasmine, God is telling me to hitch-hike." (John had hitch-hiked 7 years before he met me and he was tired of it, so God would chasten me to get his attention.) We'd cross the street, put our thumb out, and immediately get a ride... That was the ride Jesus wanted. We were exhausted from walking, very meek and quiet in that person's car, and their soul was open to us. We would listen well, and they would pour out their hearts 200 miles down the road. And we'd pray with them before we left, and we'd be closer to our next destination. That's how it would go.

Chapter 6

SERVING GOD – INSIDE OUT

Thou wilt keep him in perfect peace, whose mind is stayed on thee: because he trusteth in Thee. Trust ye in the LORD for ever: for in the LORD JEHOVAH is everlasting strength. Isaiah 26:3-4

Let's see, how do I describe our lifestyle – Giving up all to follow Jesus – Take up your cross and follow Him... Yes, there are still people that do that... And you don't have to belong to a cult to do it. Of course, the early church was called a cult by early unbelievers! But that was persecution! "But the anointing which ye have received of Him abideth in you, and ye need not that any man teach you... but as that same anointing teaches you of all things, and is truth, and is no lie, and even as it <u>hath taught you</u>, ye shall abide in Him." 1 John 2:27.

The main difference between a cult and a zealous believer is this – Nobody constrains you to do anything "Like a robot" – A cult is really like a gang, they tell you what to do, how to think, how to dress – to parrot them. And the Gang-leader is always a tyrant with a big megalomaniac complex... Although some Christians may get "cultish", or forceful in their zealousness, and of course there are "Jesus cults" – not usually even born again, as well as other religious cults – But the main thing is, nobody is holding a gun to your head with "real zeal".

In other words, out of the love of God, you suddenly <u>want</u> to serve Him with your whole heart... and nobody tells you that you must hit the road – from the outside – it is an inner experience from your living Experience with the Real Lord Jesus Christ – Because you got born again and the fire of God is in you... prompting you gently but firmly to holy resolve.

Now Voices are a big issue here – but the word of God is your guide-line and Compass and the Holy Spirit inside you – after being born again – will be the enlightener to you of the Scriptures. As it says in 1 John 2:27, "Ye need not that any man teach you, but that same anointing <u>will</u> teach you all things" ... That anointing being the Holy Spirit in Power – He then Empowers you to do whatever He wants you to do. Oh, we have Pastors and Apostles, Teachers, Evangelists, and Prophets, in the Bible, as leaders – or servants of the Lord – But a born again Christian – is both knitted to the body of Christ in a mystical way – but also autonomous – in a mystical way – Because the Holy Spirit inside you will teach you all things... This is what makes you <u>not</u> a cult... Personal Conviction – and the ability to decide on your own because of it. You know the old cliché – the pupil going up to the mountain to talk to the guru for wisdom – "Oh master tell me...?" Well, the Master or Teacher <u>is</u> the Holy Spirit through the Lord Jesus Christ and the Father in Heaven – He's inside of you – You are the recipient – "the monk" – of His holy wisdom – and others (Pastors, Apostles, Teachers, Evangelists, and Prophets) are guardians of the word of God – are just there to help you if you get stumped... or thrown off course or derailed... But <u>again</u>, the Holy Spirit will be doing the work in them – or through you. If the spiritual leader gives you faulty wisdom, the Holy Spirit <u>inside</u> of you will get checked, as it says in 1 John 2:27, <u>you need not that any man teach you</u> – will take over – and that same anointing will teach you all things – like William Penn, the Quaker, said "<u>I hate obedience unto authority without conviction</u>". Why? Because <u>not</u> every authority is cracked up to be what he or she says they are – some are false, some are back-slidden. Paul complains of this in his letters. Some are cobra snakes that spit in your eyes and blind you with false teachings or an <u>impure life</u>. Did not Jesus warn us of the "Pharisee Snake – who love the praises of men more than the praises of God," John 12:43. Some of them have <u>elevated themselves</u> – <u>not</u> God! Vainglory! Heaven is what matters, folks – not vainglory or being popular – God's Glory – "being small", so He can greatly use you – What a difference in attitude!

The point is, even if you are a newly born again babe – God doesn't want you to be gullible – believe everything any holier than thou tells you – He wants you to be, "<u>wise</u> as <u>serpents</u> <u>harmless as doves</u>," Mt. 10:16, and "test the spirits" I Jn.4:1,NIV, with your inner compass, the Holy Spirit. That's why we need to get that inner compass strong and not just rely on others to get our spiritual food – but learn to get our own. A baby eagle is fed by his mother but as soon as he gets his wings working – he gets his own food – and so we must do – <u>or we aren't growing</u>. Just as a babe grows to an adult – so must we all fulfill our Calling. As a "Babe in the woods" of Christiandome – can you get easily fooled? You certainly can – but you may be young but the Holy Spirit inside you, the Lord Jesus Christ, and Father in Heaven (the Ancient of Days), your Friend is the all wise and Eternal God – and He'll stop us – if something isn't right, <u>if</u> we prayerfully depend on Him – <u>Him alone</u> – <u>not man</u>! No – don't go to the local fortune-teller; that would be disastrous and blasphemous. Go to the Lord Jesus, prayerfully, truthfully, and humbly-if something doesn't feel right to you or "someone" doesn't. Pray and ask God for wisdom and understanding like King Solomon did.

Come all ye faithful, joyful and triumphant – Who is that song talking about? Benny Hin? John the Baptist? Pastor so-and-so? It's talking about you and I – all ye faithful – not just the big shots – but all of us who believe. Does that describe you – faithful, joyful, and triumphant? No! Then it is time you claimed your rights and became that new creature God created you to be – faithful, joyful, and triumphant. And as the song goes,

Come all ye faithful, joyful and triumphant,

Oh come ye oh come ye to Bethlehem

Oh come let us adore Him Christ the King.

And that says it all! Praising and praying to God is how to get next to the King of Kings. And reading the word of God, and repenting daily of sins – <u>even</u>, if it's just bad thoughts!

Chapter 7

FINDING THE GEMS

The hardest thing to find is often the answer... Just as Gems are buried beneath the earth and are not so easy to find, though they can be through much preparation, as in knowing where to look and endless digging – So we often must search the hardest for that which is most precious, and so we did. We searched for souls via the Holy Spirit's directive – people who had a hunger and thirst for righteousness – As it says in Jeremiah 29:13, people who search for God with all their hearts – gems – all dirty from the filth of the world – but nonetheless their desire was genuine. But our radar was Jesus – He directed us – We learned not to judge outwardly but by the Spirit. As we all know, we can't judge a book by its cover – neither can we tell who is a fine-tuned soul ready for the true gospel of Christ, just by looking at their pretty or not so pretty face... The "gems" often aren't covered in "gems" and mink stoles – often they are covered in railroad soot from a coal car with well-worn clothes and boots and mangy looking hair – After all the poor are rich in Faith, the Lord Jesus said – and so it is! ... Not that the rich aren't spiritually starving – they are often very empty! But all those props hold them up and make them feel smug – self-satisfied – and in need of nothing – like the Laodicean church in Revelations 3:14-18, as Jesus said, in fact, they were spiritually-naked, impoverished, and blind! What an indictment – and those were well-off Christians! In fact, the Holy Ghost inspired me with an acronym for luke-warm Christians, which spells smug... "S" for self-satisfied, "M" for money-mad, "U" for underestimating, and "G" for God.

But our traveling Doctor Jesus, always had the right recipe for the souls we met – and He even made house calls...!–Whether we met them under bridges or in houses – Jesus would have a word of comfort – a healing balm, or an exhortation; <u>an answer for their soul.</u>

The bottom line was people were not standing in line to see <u>us</u> – But Jesus was lining up the souls to see <u>us</u>, like dominoes, and each one was ripe for the picking – Hand-Picked by God – We would get a quickening and a fire and then the word would come forth and zero in on them like a laser and they never knew what hit them – But they knew suddenly that they believed – or they were revived to believe again – or their broken heart was healed – or their besetting sin was eradicated. And that's how Jesus works – He wants our obedience and <u>He does the rest.</u> If we are faithful – He is faithful to deliver the goods to us for the souls – whatever they need – He equips them.

You know the old saying "right time, right place" – well this was Jesus, the King of the Universe, the Living God, putting us in the right place, right time continually – dropping us off in box cars – saying to us – Get off here – Go here, Go there – And Voilá – There was that hungry or bitter Soul ready for Action – from God!

And you know what it says about hunger in the Bible proverb – "To the hungry soul ever bitter thing is sweet" Pr.27:7. So when we brought the sweetness of God, to a spiritually hungry soul who would eat anything God had for them, God's purest, sweetest, and mountain-top, honey of His word – His Living Waters – were they ever happy and satisfied!

They were starving and God gave them meat! Strong meat, and manna and the honey of His word – A Banquet for their souls – to deliver them to higher ground by getting God's favor in their lives. Manna from Heaven – Meat for their souls and honey for their spirits.

That was a bargain meal at a bargain price – "Freely you receive so freely you give." Any time we thought we were on vacation – we would be hanging out for three days under a bridge – twiddling our thumbs – God would hinder us or delay us – stop us cold – John would say by the third day, "just when I think I'm on a vacation – that's when God shows me I'm not." Then two or three hours later along would come a soul at that very bridge, sometimes two or three souls – The conversation would begin and we would feel that holy fire and would ignite what started out as a mundane chat, would turn into a soul-searching, soul-wrenching conversation. We seldom said anything to start it – it was <u>God</u> – He was there! Suddenly one man would say out of the blue, "I sure thank God all the time he saved my a**" Bam! And off it would go... freewheeling, naked talk, no masks – all heart – and God was there with Divine fellowship –We'd end up all of us, like on that rainy night in Klamath Falls, Oregon – sleeping under the same overpass after our fellowship together, lined up like sardines in the heavy rainstorm though plenty of room, singing songs of praise to Jesus under the bridge, like "Amazing Grace", "Rock of Ages", "Because He Lives", "How Great Thou Art", our favorite songs that we all knew from our childhood – 'til we fell asleep and feeling God's presence and angels, putting us all to sleep in sweet fellowship in cold weather.

Next morning me and my husband John, slipped down a path to relieve ourselves in the early morning – We came back and the three or four men were back on the bottom of the bridge talking in an animated way – Then they pointed at us and laughed – "What?" We said! They replied, "Oh we all wondered where you went – We thought for sure you were angels and disappeared!" We answered, "We wish! Praise the Lord!" What a compliment! All because we followed the presence of God to <u>where He wanted to manifest</u> amongst the meek and lowly – railroad "wayfarers" – He was meeting them in the highways and byways as the Scriptures say and saying "come on into my feast" – as other people are too busy from their middle-class appointments and elite echelons to hear my Word – "Blessed are the meek for they shall inherit the Earth," Matthew 5:5. And Jesus also said in Matthew 11:28-30 "Come unto me, all who labor and are heavy laden, and I will give you rest. Take my yoke upon you, and learn of me for I am meek and lowly in heart: and ye shall find rest unto your souls. For my yoke is easy and my burden is light," and so He did!

Chapter 8

MEEKNESS ISN'T WEAKNESS

Yes, meekness was a part of Jesus, a lot of people prefer to overlook – of course, meekness is not weakness – as I well can testify to.

I remember one amazing time in Texas when we met a smooth talking Texas older woman who pastored a church in Texas. She was spooning out what we call that "ice cream and candy" gospel or that's what the Lord called it to us. She was telling them what they wanted to hear – get rich quick schemes and all – and oh she was saying Jesus only wanted you to be rich and he didn't call people to live out doors and be degraded like that. "Nooo" she said in a Texas drawl – as she looked glaringly at me and John with appalling audacity, as if to tar and feather us for our outlandish backpacks and dirty faces, as we just got off the freight train. "Jesus," she said "wants you to be rich and have plenty and be satisfied. That's the blessing of God," she nearly hissed and said with a smug and obvious nod – our way. Well we sat there and took it all in as meek as lambs, all tuckered out – and the Spirit of the Lord came upon my husband and I and showed us that she was a "Pharisee snake" and liked to preach money so that she would get plenty of money to fill her oversized fat pockets – So we waited until she was done downgrading us and saying how cursed of God we, the poor, were; and then when all the people were getting ready to leave and filing out – we quietly approached her – I heard my husband say to her "my wife and I are tramps for Jesus – He called us to walk, hitch-hike, ride the freight trains, and preach the gospel on the railroad freight trains to tramps – and that's our Calling." "That's right," I said. "God uses the weak things and the despised things to bring to nought the wise and crafty" – 1 Corinthians 3:18-19-21. 1 Corinthians 1:26-29.

"Oh," she said with real venom – "my Jesus was no bum." My husband and I said, "foxes have holes and birds of the air have nests but the son of man has nowhere to lay his head." Mt.8:20, – that was Jesus!" "Oh, my Jesus was no bum," she says again more fiercely with a Texas drawl dragging it out. "But Jesus <u>was</u> meek and lowly," my husband John said – she spit it out this time with anger – "My Jesus was no bum!!" Then John continued, "He <u>was</u> meek and lowly – and you are a "Pharisee snake," that's what Jesus told us about you!" Matthew 23:1-33. I readily agreed! And the word of God went into her like fire slowly and powerfully and we walked away and we knew God's word doesn't return void. Knowing the word of the Lord would do the work on her she needed most! Hallelujah "a prophet's work is never done! And it's a thankless job," my husband would always say – and we'd laugh! And we'd be on our way. She was really getting on in years and we were <u>sent</u> to tell her that – God would work her overtime now! We knew that from experience.

Chapter 9

TAKING YOUR TIME; READY – SET – GO! HOBO TALENT UNVEILED

On the road we learned to take our time. We'd get all that bourgeois speed out of us! We had to as it may be a matter of life or death – Our energy level is slowed down, but we were carrying a big backpack and all we needed to do was take it slow – and think – But then we were always ready like a waiting Bengal tiger to spring into action and go when the Lord would tell us to, Ready – Set – Go! It's conserved energy – utilized to the max in the awesome challenge of survival!

In some towns we would wait 14 hours sometimes for a freight train to arrive – but then it would take us 500 miles – It was worth it – we were waay slowed down for 14 hours of waiting – then an adrenaline rush of catching that train right on time – getting out of those yards safely, incognito, and being free as a bird as we sped down the tracks looking at the scenery – sometimes quite beautiful! What an experience! What joy, what exhilarating fun! We had – my darling and I. Yes the lowly life of hobos was transforming. When I met my husband at 37, hitch-hiking for Jesus, he had very short hair. After all, he grew up in the Elvis Presley era, born in 1940, and used to call the hippies "girls" who had long hair, but the Lord Jesus rebuked him for that in a vision in the 1970s, and after 12 years of riding the freight trains, from 1981-1991 and off and on after that until 2001 – John had a beard and longish hair.

It's funny when people have wealth; the pharisaical elitist attitude is to fear that awful "dark" being living out doors outside on the streets and under bridges or in the boonies. Well it's true there are some "dangerous" elements – like fugitives from the law – but what the elite set forget is that Jesus chose to dwell amongst the <u>meek</u> and <u>lowly</u> mainly because the high-minded elite pharisaical types were the more dangerous element and did indeed incite the crowds to crucify Him. Jesus also called Himself meek and lowly! In fact, the Pharisees rebuked Jesus for hanging out with <u>those sinners</u>, Mark 2:16-17, and indicated at one point that the "poor" were the lawless and unruly ones – unlearned! Yet the learned scribes and Pharisees were usually <u>more</u> beastly and treacherous with <u>real</u> lawless behavior. As the middle class, (as we once were), are taught to fear the common, lowly, ordinary man who was a threat to the status quo. Why? Because deep down the insecure bourgeois have a <u>fear</u> of losing it all – and becoming like that poor, unfortunate person who has the task of being the scapegoat for society, especially those dirty railroad tramps. It is survival – survival of the fittest – keeping the poor man down, to keep their illusion of grandeur and superiority in tact; and thus appear invincible... Which nobody is!

And we always notice – the ones that screamed as they drove by in their cars, "Get a job, bum!" as we walked by in our "despicable" backpacks, were the ones that were one step away from being there themselves, usually – more the petite bourgeois or lower middle class. These were people hanging on to some loathsome job by the skin of their teeth while they drank their way to oblivion at night – wondering when they'd be axed for their unhappy behavior in the morning after exhaustion in a boring nowhere job. Well, that's how we saw it anyway, and that's how Jesus showed it to us. People who are afraid of the lowly always forget, the <u>more</u> money you have, the <u>more</u> evil you can do. The math is simple. So don't pick on us – Thank you!

I well remember the time we rode on a freight train, past a warehouse dock, in the outskirts of a California town. The men were right out on the deck loading fruit in boxes. We stood in a wide open boxcar, observing, as the train went by very slowly – thinking they'd be amused to see a couple of freight train riders, as people often are and even would wave at us! But suddenly they barraged us with fruit, really aiming to hit us hard – we ducked and ducked and dodged, but the lemons that came right at us, too fast, stopped just short of hitting us – And I really felt the Spirit of the Lord protecting us – but I know they hoped they'd hit us! Why? What did we do to them? We were free! That's what! It's the price you pay for freedom! And they were jealous – stuck in a daily grind they hadn't wanted – or bargained for.

That's why Jesus says, "Come unto me all ye that are laboring and heavy laden <u>and I will give you rest</u>. Take my yoke upon you and learn of me, for I am meek and lowly in heart..." Mt.11:28-29. He, the Lord Jesus, gives a person hope even if they are strapped for cash, and <u>in a job they hate</u> – <u>He gives us hope in all circumstances</u> – The Lord Jesus is our beacon of light who can buffer us from hard circumstances, and make all the difference in attitude because He is Heavenly Light and He knows we are but dust and empty without Him, whether struggling in a factory job to pay rent or living in Bel Air with maid servants in a mansion on a lonely hill!

Chapter 10

THE BROKEN-HEARTED

The Broken-Hearted are often the most prone to being left behind, left out and ostracized – not always maliciously so – But because their body language portrays a soul that just doesn't care! That's shrinking from contact.

It's kind of a healing place to be actually – if the person isn't rushed or abused by anyone – even Jesus says, "Blessed are they that mourn for they shall be comforted." And Eccles. 7:2-4, says, "It is better to be in the house of mourning than in the house of mirth." On the other hand it says – "Woe unto you who laugh now – for you shall weep." Beatitudes, St. Luke 6:20-26, St. Matthew 5:3-12

Now there is healthy healing laughter – and raucous, empty laughter and that's the kind He is talking about. Like raccoons foraging in the night for free scraps of food, the soul often when desperately wicked and empty will search for any tidbits of glamour or fun to party up those empty dead spaces inside and laugh, but all the soul is doing that's filled with the garbage of the world – is throwing the same old garbage around with hilarity but in a different form – comedy. But now is that soul relieved after or revived? No... it's just a fix – a temporary fix of relief from sordid thoughts and sordid deeds. The Bible calls it debauchery, one of the deeds of the flesh. It's like putting a band-aid over a huge festering wound – it would do no good!

But there is Joyous laughter – or self-revealing laughter, that comes from after a time of sorrow – or from sorrowful experiences. Many comedians are funny because of their deep sufferings. Sometimes even the "funnies" gave me a good laugh as a widow when I was low.

In the grief of losing my spouse of 28 years – I <u>could</u> rush out and look for a party time and escape – but that would be more depressing to me – and I <u>am</u> a Christian. But I can watch these little jaybirds by the tent and they are so filled with antics, picking up the bread and dropping it – then trying to carry more than one piece – two or three times and dropping it again – they make me laugh! It is innocent laughter and it's healing – When we would be with our homeless friends on the railroad, often heart-broken people – Strangers though we were, somehow in sorrows being expressed openly – we'd all end up laughing and God would turn our mourning into joy… It was amazing how much more I could laugh out there, than in a stilted erudite setting where everyone minds their manners and no one expresses their grief or mistakes – even in some churches it gets that way, sad to say – everyone being plastic-fantastics as the hippies used to say. Well, that's how it was with the poorest of the poor, the traveling Wayfarers – no masks – or guarded faces – just real Koinia fellowship and love. When you have true fellowship – You have salt – and when you have salt – you have Fire! God visits you and you may even have to sing "Kumbya my Lord! Kumbya."

Like Jesus said in Matthew 5:13, "Ye are the salt of the earth" and just as people laugh the most at salty comedians who shock us with the truth – Jesus tells us who believe, not to lose our own salt or it will be trampled on – meaning our words will be ineffective. For example, the prophet Samuel was commended by the Lord as a young man, that none of his words fell to the ground, 1 Samuel 3:19 – he was full of salt! He was filled with the Holy Ghost and fire! When you're filled with God – you speak the <u>truth</u> and you don't care what people think as long as God gives you the green light to say it. Like my husband, John, as a Prophet, in his Calling, (as am <u>I</u> also), he would often offend people by his bluntness, but he was able to cut through to their inner core – because God told him to say it. He was a yielded vessel and he'd say it. Even if they got spittin' mad. Salty words bring healthy mourning when inspired by the Lord Jesus and cause the spirit of the person to repent. Salty words are not just being blunt and offensive to everyone, like "hello, you look fat and ugly today". Love covers sin and faults, <u>at times</u> – especially when it's obvious – you can speak the truth with salt when you do it for integrity's sake, for righteousness sake – like standing up for the weak and poor or rebuking a tyrant, or setting a captive free. Salty words can also bring laughter as you admit the truth about yourself or others in a way that sets others free. God taught my husband and me when a person's sin was obvious; <u>to speak beyond their sin,</u> because they were already humbled <u>by</u> their sin, but God would use us to rebuke people who were <u>wise</u> in their own <u>conceit</u> and <u>arrogant in</u> their sins, Proverbs 26:5&12.

Nathaniel was another example – the Lord Jesus commended him for speaking without guile – first insulting Jesus' birthplace, "Nazareth," but then boldly confessing Jesus as the Son of God. Nathaniel had salt, St. John 1:45-51, and even received a gift of discerning of spirits because of it – seeing "angels ascending and descending upon the Son of Man."

So, if you find yourself laughing too much over too little, maybe it's time you get in the house of mourning and do some serious soul-searching – praying – or reading the Bible. Some people need to spend time alone – <u>not</u> escape reality through entertainment, then they can face whatever is really bothering them or who? Or Face God!

Chapter 11
Solace

Out there in the boonies – riding the freight trains – clipping along the railroad tracks in town after town – through the mountains, past the rivers and deserts and canyons and oceans – we can have plenty of time for solace – and we learned to value it and to be refreshed. It was a habit of solace so we could refresh others eventually as well. It's no wonder – society has AA meetings and grief hospices, etc. There's hardly anywhere you can go to be <u>real</u> anymore – obviously some go to the bar to get open – but that can be addictive and demoralizing, and demonizing and cause worse problems as well. If you don't have any identifiable problem in <u>society</u> – you're up a creek – and it's hard to talk to anyone. And even church at times turns into stilted social clubs – how about we have "Relief Centers"? – just places to go to relieve your woes – You don't have to be an alcoholic or mentally ill person or grieving a loss or be addicted to food, or a teenager, or a drug taker, or a senior – no special label – just relief – wouldn't that be lovely – free of charge – hospitable haven – for "whoever". Well no one would support such a vague notion, would they – But one relief center we can go to is the Lord Jesus Christ – and He is our "ever present help in time of trouble". He will not laugh raucously at our troubles, as some do, or tell us to have another double – He will listen with great tender-loving-care and give us the truth that will set us free – any believer who knows Jesus – can become a Relief Center – as long as we follow Him faithfully and live holy lives – pretty soon the seed of the Kingdom of God will grow into a huge tree and people will want to lodge under your tree for shade and relief – under the Shadow of the Almighty – in your life too! You'll be a walking Relief Center – wherever you go.

Chapter 12
OUTWARD APPEARANCE

While riding the freight trains, John my husband really let his hair grow – he pulled all stops out of trying to look bourgeois. It was in his nature, or rather his era, to have short hair – as he was 14 ½ years older than I, when I met him at 37 years old in 1978. He was born in 1940, the "Elvis era" more than the Beetles long-hair era. I would cut his hair using one finger for width measurement, as that's how short it was, and he wore polyester brown pants and short-sleeved white shirts with little dotty stars all over them – very conservative. When you saw him hitch-hiking he wasn't very rough looking at all – kind of priestly or like a business man. Me, I personally like long hair on men as that was my era. I was born in 1954. John was born in 1940! He told me how Jesus rebuked him in a vision, not to give the hippies a hard time (which he did) and that someday he'd have long hair too. So he stopped calling them "girls" and saying "does not nature itself even say men shouldn't have long hair" and he behaved himself as he was running into a lot of "Jesus people" hippie groups and even grew his hair a little below the collar line when on a long journey. Well eventually – he cut loose and it was the freight trains that really relaxed him and me too, as well, the Lord Jesus releasing us to be totally at ease. He started to wear blue jeans or tougher pants and he let his hair get longer and it was naturally wavy and looked very dashing, I thought – and he had his goatee and a mustache. I thought it was great! But John, really had to die to his flesh – it was an abasement to him – to not be so conservative. John was from back east after all, Pittsburgh, Pennsylvania.

For example, we'd be walking along, and along would drive by some real red-necks in many small country conservative towns all over the United States, and they'd scream "Hey hippie. Get a job!" at the top of their voice. John would turn and look at me shocked. "Who are they talking to?" he'd say. "You, dear. I'm afraid it's you and me!" I would say, amused. I just love John – he was such a loving, kind brother – we had a relationship we could talk about anything – Anyway that was one thing he had to die to in the Lord Jesus abasement program for our lives. The other thing was the word "bum". That was hard for John to take and me, too. We'd say "Hey, we're not bums. We work," at first. But eventually when we were on our missionary calling we learned to die to our pride and stop defending ourselves – Eventually we got over our defensiveness about the "work" question and we said to a cop one time, "I'm not afraid to work and I'm not afraid <u>not</u> to work," (as the Holy Spirit taught us to). And he said, "I'm a sociology major as well, and that is great because that is a common problem people have. And <u>I'm</u> afraid <u>not</u> to work, myself." Like we read in the popular book about a couple who walked across America – called "Walking Across America," I believe, a hitch-hiker doesn't like to be called a "bum" – because actually a bum is someone who is homeless but stays in one place and a tramp is the word used by the freight train riders, (formerly hobos – which actually came from the words hoe-boy during the Depression, when they'd hop a freight train and carry a hoe, usually with a little sack of belongings, to show they were willing to work) – and hitch-hikers really don't like to be called tramps, though they are tramping it as we found out! – But freight train riders embrace the word tramp – So we'd say we were tramps for the Lord Jesus Christ but not "bums", but eventually decided to embrace the word "bum"(as people would yell that at us) – much like African-Americans embrace the n-word to take the sting out of it, amongst each other. So to make people's flesh crawl, John would say – "Yes, I'm a bum for Jesus!" Ha-ha. Quite a stir – and yes we stood up in congregations and said that – when they <u>asked</u> for our testimony – the <u>reason</u> for the <u>joy</u> on our faces they could <u>visibly</u> see – (Baptists, Methodist, Pentecostals, Lutherans, Charismatic Catholics, etc.) – or why they could feel the "anointing", <u>was</u> our <u>consecrated</u> lives. And we didn't even have to promote ourselves. Psalm 37:3-7, Psalm 75:5-7

When John and I got to a Baptist church for the first time in Northern California, I well remember his opening line as he met the pastor at the door – 15 minutes before the service. "Do you let bums worship here who love Jesus?" His mouth would drop and then he'd study us with our backpacks and John's longish hair and me beside him like a good soldier 5'2" and John 5'11", "well" he'd say, "well, you are welcome," and ask us a few pertinent theological questions and next thing you know he'd say, "would you give your testimony here in this congregation this morning?" "Sure" we'd say and he replied, "I'll introduce you and you stand up to tell people how Jesus uses you just like you told me." And that would be that – kaboom – we'd be extremely abased and suddenly be exalted – telling forty or fifty people or so, about Jesus in our lowly life. "He that exalts himself shall be humbled – but he that humbles himself shall be exalted." Matthew 23:12 NIV

When John and I were betrothed in the summer of 1978, we were a <u>seasoned blend</u> for life, (28 years), consummated and consecrated and being on the road was our lifelong honeymoon – it nearly lasted a lifetime! Praise God! How sweet it was! And how sweet it is to be loved by Jesus in lowliness and meekness – Our relationship with Jesus was pure as He truly called us to the road, and in order to be <u>protected</u> we knew we had to <u>stay</u> prayed-up, because our lives were always at risk. Our relationship with each other was disciplined. We learned <u>not</u> to fight, to get along – to fight <u>only</u> to keep the peace and to be open and honest with each other – because again, you <u>are</u> risking your neck and like good soldiers, and we knew there is a greater battle at stake than fighting each other – And neither me nor John liked to fight – so we got along with Jesus' help – keeping us One – for the Lord Jesus Christ put us together. John was the husband I finally had the sense to pray for, as I got <u>saved</u> at almost 22, and I had met him at 23. He was indeed a long lost brother, lover, and best friend for 28 years of our arduous but exciting life as "Tramps for Jesus".

Chapter 13

LIFE IS NOT A GAME OF CHANCE

Life is not a game of Chance—"It is a measurement—and with what measure you mete it shall be measured to you again." Matthew 7:2.

Everything you do is measured by God and the choices you make affect your whole life–some call it a ripple effect—So when we're out there for the Lord Jesus Christ and He truly called us—it was no game of chance—It was a miracle! God protected us and inspired us every step of the way—" for precept must be upon precept, precept upon precept; line upon line, line upon line; here a little, and there a little."—He did it! Isaiah 28:9-10

We did not just happen to be there for that soul—It was God! Wouldn't you want to have your life measured out by God! Well He did it for us—so it can be done. And He did it for those souls we encountered with perfect ripe fruit timing for their lives.

We're His apostles, His golden sold-out children, led by the strong arm of the Lord Jesus—Guiding us, leading us and sending us to His dark hidden places, where people were dwelling in a sub-culture of freedom and personal adventure of survival—living in the great outdoors, in places we called—nowhere. But nonetheless—it had its merits—Some places, we slept under bridges—but other places we slept under cliffs overlooking the ocean, or by beautiful rivers with forests surrounding us—Places where people of higher echelons would pay to have Banquets for a wedding party—or pay beau-coupé bucks to live there! How ironic! Every tramp knows what I'm talking about—it's the "King of the Road" theme! Remember that song? "Ain't got no cigarettes but I'm King of the Road"—it was sung by Roger Miller in the '60s. Well it was one of the few adult songs I bothered to remember as a kid... And I must say—it came back clearly as I sailed along the beautiful mountains from Klamath Falls to Eugene, Oregon—with my beloved husband—viewing the view from our wide open box car door—bigger than any Amtrak window—What a site to see—What a miraculous God we serve who created all this beauty.

Time stood still when you travel via freight train—You could just relax... and take in the view—not a care in the world—It was healing to the soul...it was being in the care of the awesome God—in His Hand—under the shadow of the Almighty—Who could tell when we'd be coming that way again—we were moving in the Spirit and God was with us—Jehovah Jira—Our Provider—<u>His faith is Sufficient for me</u>!

(Song) *Hallelujah, yes I'm walking with the King, praise His Holy Name—Every day the same—Hallelujah, yes I'm walking with the King, Every day I'm walking with the King. Now the Devil doesn't like us cause we're walking with the King. Praise His Holy Name... Every day the same!*

Chapter 14
FAITH

The Poor are Rich in Faith
(The more you have the less secure you are)
Matthew 6:25-26
1. Take no thought for your life
2. What to eat or what to drink
3. Nor yet for your body what to put on.
Conclusion: Is not life more than meat, and the body more than clothes.
Ex. Behold: The fowls (birds) of the air
Consider—they don't sow, nor reap, nor gather into barns
Gathering into barns seemed to be standard for riches—(ex. rich man who said I will fill up my barns for surplus. Luke 12:18-21,22-28.)
But the Heavenly Father takes care of them and feeds them.
Conclusion: How much more shall He take care of you!
Through anxiety you cannot add even an inch to your height—
So why worry about your attire
Ex. Consider—the lilies of the field in growing
They do not toil (work) or spin (clothes)
But Solomon in all his glory was not arrayed like one of these.
Wherefore if God clothes the grass of the field which lasts a day and another may be cast into fire
How much more shall He cloth you—oh ye of little faith.

Well, as you know the poor are rich in faith—Jesus says so through James 2:5. Why does he say this, you may ask, if you're not poor—doesn't that feel like a low blow—Well He has a very good reason—When you're poor as opposed to having plenty—you stop putting faith in things and put your faith—very possibly in the invisible—It's the Spiritual law—the less you have the more faith in God you have—The more you have—the less you are secure—When a rich man suddenly loses it all—he may kill himself—(It happened in the 1920s stock market crash)—Why? Because he has no faith in God—that's the invisible God who made Heaven and earth and takes care of the birds and the lilies who will deliver that suddenly poor rich man in the time of need—that's Jesus who died on the cross for his/her sins and will not let him perish if he just humbles himself and calls out to the living God for help. Often times, the rich man's pride and identity are all wrapped up in those "things" he or she lost as a treasure on earth—not in Heaven. That's why the Bible says, "Take heed and beware of covetness for man's life <u>does not consist in the abundance of things he possesses,</u>" Luke 12:15 – So it goes <u>the Lord Jesus knew what was in the heart of man and understood his weakness for materialism, which is a form of idolatry, which can become a form of self-idolatry.</u>

For Example: Gary is known by his yacht... and his golf pro trophies and his jet set friends, and his two mansions—<u>But does anybody know the real "Gary"</u>...Wait... not even his wife? No, she's off living an independent life with her jet-set friends and impressing them, and could care less what makes Gary tick anymore. After the first affair and second and third she lost interest—not to mention a few of her own. How about his dog? Yes, Rex knows Gary because Gary pours his heart out to his dog because Rex won't talk—he is safe. So it goes man's best friend is his dog—especially when he doesn't know to turn to God Almighty with his problems—the Great problem solver, and in his reluctance to being alone—talking to his dog instead. But as that old radio show theme goes, the "Shadow knows," the shadow could be God, and He understands Gary down to the core—He's just waiting quietly for Gary to crack and humble himself to Him, not his dog—but to Him, God Almighty. Then Gary will get some answers—but that pride, that damn rich man's pride won't let him. Like it said in the movie *Wall Street*, for the rich men that played the stocks—"Wasps—they love animals, hate people." And even God gets forgotten too.

(Song) *Standing in the Shadows, you'll find Jesus and you'll know Him by the nail prints in His hands.*

You see Gary is an actor. He's learned to act all his life—and put on the happy, charming face to everyone—he might cry over his beer a little when no one is looking—but he's so good at acting he fools himself... this is the danger of deception. Some day we might just believe our own mask—when we need God the most—it all boils down to one thing—If you have a burden of sin that is too great to bare—get in your closet and pray to God—the Lord Jesus Christ and find out if He really cares—that's why He's called our Savior! Regarding rich men, even Jesus said," With men this is impossible; but with God all things are possible." Matthew 19:26

Chapter 15

Not <u>Act</u> Holy—<u>Be</u> Holy

Hypocrites are called snakes, like the Pharisees Jesus was always picking on, after they attacked Him viciously. Why? Because they pretended to be holy—but they were only <u>acting</u> holy—putting on long faces and showing off when they fasted—Oh fasting sounds holy and all, but did they Love God—No, Jesus said they wanted the praises of men more than the praises of God. Jesus—never acted—He was Himself—He was God—He didn't Act Holy... <u>He was Holy</u>. He wants us to "<u>be holy</u>"—Not <u>act</u> holy. I Peter 1:16

When I was first on the road—I tried too hard sometimes to act tough—fearing certain kinds of predatory types, Jesus would say to me in a still small voice, "don't 'act' tough—'be' tough". Or I would suddenly be in a big Church that Jesus sent me to and I was aware of people's judgment of our "dirty clothes and faces"—just coming off a freight train. I would try to "act" religious. Jesus would say to me—"don't <u>act</u> holy, <u>be</u> holy." So then I understood—I was living a holy life... I just had to maintain my stance—not compromise to anyone's crude suggestions—and not back down in my confession of faith. Then, I knew Jesus would radiate His already indwelling presence through my face—with my <u>holy life</u>, as I testified of Him. Not everyone would agree with me—but when you take off your mask—everyone knows you're for real, even when it makes their flesh crawl... A radiant, holy life cannot be despised—Some will be offended but that's good, other's convicted, and others supremely blessed—It all comes out in the wash—the wash of the Holy Ghost. And He doesn't white-wash things—He's for real and will get to your real core—so watch out—Get around a Spirit-filled Christian and challenge their faith and He'll come at you like Zorro with the sword of truth and your costume and mask will be on the floor as you stand naked—in God's Room—as the truth sets you free—spoken by anointed vessels of clay...

Now for the poor—the poor man is stripped already—he realizes he has to depend on what is inside—not on the outside—to survive. He has to be real to even be heard. He is a nobody to society. So what's he got to lose—humility is not a disguise—it's facile—easy to be entreated. A proverb says in the Bible, "A rich man is wise in his own conceit, but a poor man *who has understanding* searches him out." Proverbs 28:11

Also it says, "The poor useth entreaties; but the rich answereth roughly." Prv.18:23

Isn't that true... people like to think the poor are crude—well some can be, but isn't the man who sneers at you, if you get in his way or cuts you off in the middle of your sentence, because he has more important things to do, (he thinks).

John, my husband—was a poor man who would sit quietly and be content with not being noticed—until some elite person just had to ask him about the peace of God in his life—and then he'd tell them. It happened all the time. He knew from experience to ignore the rich elite people he was with. He already knew their thoughts that they thought they were better than him—you see the poor man searched them out.

Chapter 16

Love Lifted Me

There's nothing quite like love to revive us when we have disharmony. This whole world is in disharmony, heading to hell in a hand-basket, – filled with selfishness and divisiveness, contentions with other countries – contentions even in our own countries and households – rivalries, slander, deceit, greed, murder, witchcraft – you name it, we've done it – the whole human race.

So Jesus comes along – Big Savior – full of Love – God incarnate – in a human vessel. He survives the test of being human. He, being God, but trapped in a human body overcomes the rancid effects of sin and remains perfect so He can die for our sins with perfect sacrifice and be resurrected – so we can also die to our sins and be resurrected in Him! – The Lord Jesus Christ is our lifeboat in this sordid world – our only hope to get to Heaven… I want to go to Heaven – Don't you? Jesus was and is the perfect Sacrifice. What God the Father did in giving up His only begotten Son, is Eternal and the Holy Spirit enters our hearts, as well, when we receive Jesus in our heart as Lord and Savior, repenting of our sins. The Godhead comes and homesteads in us – makes a dwelling in our temple of clay – we become <u>like</u> Jesus though we're not perfect – but striving towards perfection, as our old nature of sins slowly fall off like dead leaves on us. And He puts his revival in our hearts daily and so we must seek Him daily – though saved – for this life of <u>eternal merit</u>.

There is wrong merit and right merit – a lot of people strive for wrong merit – to be bigger and stronger than those other wimps out there – to beat up the most people or to engage in the most lovers, or to be deceitful and fooling people, con-artists, or to be the cleverest thief on the block, to be the best swindler, or to hate the most people like hate groups do. Such merit – has it's carnal rewards, but it is really merit-less. What really counts is merit – not done for the egomaniacal self – and some people by stealth do meritous good things, but disguised entirely with selfish motives behind it. But what counts is merit done for <u>Love</u> – <u>Eternal Merit</u> – and <u>God is Love</u>. 1 Corinthians 13, 1 John 4:8

I know my husband had great Eternal Merit – he really suffered with an ileostomy from 24 years of age – no large intestine at all, but a bag on his side – he obeyed an arduous Calling at 30 years old to backpack it on foot and hitch-hike all over the United States for 7-8 years, before he met me. And for 28 years we continued this journey together. What guts and courage it took John to do this and all for the love of Jesus. He lived totally by faith – there was no "disability check" for him. His testimonies were awesome when I met him and I never ceased loving such a pure, loving man. Jesus had transformed him from a selfish human being to a man that literally lay down his life for the brethren. In the end he was hated by some, persecuted and martyred – serving the Lord Jesus Christ faithfully – mostly on the road, his poor body wore out, and treacherous souls who despised him, cost him heartbreak and sickness that landed him on dialysis in the end. But Jesus embraced him into eternal glory and thank God John had many healthy years on the road for Jesus. Different pastors from entirely different churches would lay hands on my husband two years before he was Called and get the same word of the Lord that he would be a seasoned traveler who would travel anywhere for Jesus and *any way* and suffer a lot of hardship on the road. They would cry and weep over him with the same message, amazingly they didn't know that Katherine Kuhlman had prophesied that same Calling over him, when John was 12 years old, and first got saved and knocked down by the power of God. Such is the Call of God, and such is the power of God's love, binding lost souls. His treasures found by the living Lord Jesus! – being recovered from the snare of the devil, with God's Perfect Love, made into an entirely new creature, as they weep over their sins and discover – the Perfect Reflection of God, through Jesus Christ in their lives.

Jesus finds the eternal forgotten seed – that is buried in all of us – and as we weep for our sinful nature – that seed is watered and grows as Jesus enters our hearts. The Husbandman, Lord Jesus nurtures our young seedling into a beautiful huge tree, that eventually, some day the birds (souls) will find shade under, and its leaves will not wither, and its roots will go down deep to reach many Lives for Jesus and Eternity!!! Matthew 13:31,32 & Psalm 1:3

As the old song goes:

I was sinking deep in sin, far from the peaceful shores, very deeply staying within, sinking to rise no more, but the Master of the sea heard my despairing cry – from the waters lifted me –Now safe am I!
Love lifted me – Love lifted me – when nothing else could help – Love lifted me – Love lifted me –when nothing else could help – Love lifted me.
Souls in danger – look above – Jesus completely Saves – He will lift you by his Love – out of the angry waves – Love so mighty and so true merits my soul's best song – faithful loving service to Him, belong!
Love lifted me...

Let "Love", for God is Love – lift you out of this chaotic sordid world.

Chapter 17

TIME

Isn't it about time to say – "Stop the world I want to get off!" – long enough to get saved and filled with God's Holy Spirit, of course. I believe – we will be <u>fulfilled</u> with God's love, which is <u>perfect</u> – don't you? The Heavenly Father is waiting for us to recognize that He is the perfect Giver of love in the form of His perfect Son, Jesus Christ – the perfect Sacrifice for our sins. Time is ticking – we all gotta die. Some die fast, some die slow, (some happy, some sad), but "we all gotta die", as my husband John used to say in referring to dying to yourself, as well. That's what's really hard. The "time" bomb, you might call it... it will explode – the day you die! And it will bring us into eternal damnation, <u>Hell</u>, or Eternal Glory, <u>Heaven</u>. The window of time will close and the window of Eternity will open wherever we go.

"Heaven is a beautiful place – filled with His glory and grace – I <u>want</u> to see Jesus' face – Oh Heaven is a beautiful place" as the song goes.

I had a solid 28 years of eternal glory in my Calling in Christ Jesus, with my husband, I will never regret – vigilant, wonderful years, of waiting on souls and being there for the right person at the right time – to lift that soul out of the mire of sin and despair... and I will continue our adventure, as God leads me on my alone path of celibacy, thus far, running the race for Jesus – being his bond-slave for His love and eternal glory.

As it says in Psalm 116:15, "Precious in the eyes of the Lord are the death of His saints" – And so I am spurred on by the death of my loved one, John- "for the blood of the martyrs is the seed of the church" as a Godly person noted.

Mercy and Love, Mercy and Love, will always thrive in the heat of battle – But none knows better than our Savior – the cost of a priceless, loving life – prevailing in a sinful world and though we appear to *fail* when we die, as in crucified, or murdered, or tossed aside, or in sickness, we are victorious to our Lord Jesus Christ as the sweet perfume of our lives permeates to those who remain on Earth, with conviction or serenity, depending on their condition.

Hallelujah! For this great adventure does end – but not for long, for we *will* see our Heavenly Eternal Friend, Jesus, and our loved ones in Him too, if we persevere in knowing Him. Hallelujah, Hallelujah – for the price is love – and the cost is life, and the truth will set us free – for eternity! "For our light affliction is but for a moment and worketh for us a far more exceeding and eternal weight of glory." 2 Corinthians 4:17

Jesus Paid it All… the Prize in the High Calling is what I seek to attain to Eternal Glory – I intend to rocket off to Eternal fame – down here – to be one of the stars that shines forever and ever. As it says in Phillippians 2:15-16, NIV, "…to become blameless and pure children of God without fault in a crooked and depraved generation, in which we shine like stars in the universe – as we hold out the word of life" – to a dying world.

And this is true uniqueness – for as it says a little farther down – "for all seek their own, not things which are Jesus Christ's" Philippians 2:21. That means, if we get out of our <u>selfish</u> <u>Self</u>, and follow Jesus, He will make each of us our unique authentic person we were meant to be, as we're all made in the image of God.

My husband – shines as a star in the universe now – and he shined as a star down here! As a nobody for Jesus who worshipped a great Somebody. Power is hidden in meekness, but <u>meekness</u> is <u>not weakness</u> – as I once read. I would rather be out chasing God's rainbows and be His vigilant star with His power and strength hidden in meekness. As it says in Daniel 12:3, "we who are wise will be like the brightness of the heavens and those that turn many to righteousness as the stars forever and ever." So the "time" bomb is waiting! Kaboom! Are we ready?

Chapter 18

PLUMBLINE

Don't be thrown by the word plumbline – it's just a measurement – I'm not good on math myself – but it's fairly simple… and it's mentioned in Amos 7:7, referring to a building measurement metaphor for our lives. God pulls the plumbline of judgment and finds the children of Israel are in serious trouble. And so the prophet of Amos spells out God's judgment to them… even if you feel as carefree as a drunken sailor on land (sorry sailor stereotype there) – there is no telling when God may require your soul. There is the rich man parable that Jesus spoke of – who is going to store up all his goodies in the barn. And what does God say – "You fool, this night your soul will be required of you!" Luke 12:17-20. Isn't it shocking? – He was smug and satisfied, but he wasn't said to be sick, probably in perfect health, feeling so arrogant – But God cut the silver cord that very night. He can do that – He's God – so we must be ready and not perish in darkness but continually labor to turn our soul to the light with continued repentance – introspection, as in "examining ourselves" in prayers without ceasing. It happens! – the nights the lights went out of Georgia – might be any of us when the lights go out for our life on Earth – best we know – the "Light of the world," the <u>Lord Jesus Christ</u>, or the lights will go out to eternal darkness forever, and we don't want to experience that – I know I don't. Praise the Lord Jesus! – we have victory over death, through our faith in the Lord Jesus Christ our Savior, our Eternal hope – who sanctions a plumbline to show mercy, if we have sought His covering of blood and pledged our allegiance to the Lord Jesus Christ, daily, forever. When we reject him who died for us, we give ourselves no mercy seat – no power to make it to Heaven – let's face it Friends – we need a Sponsor, Jesus our Lord and Savior who will take us by the hand to our Heavenly home. We need <u>His</u> sanction, as our own means <u>nothing</u> – Amen! Otherwise the plumbline will show the judgment of God and we don't want that! Yikes! "Heaven" forbid!

Chapter 19

DEATH

There are times I face death – in numerous ways – even before the death of my husband, when the Lord Jesus Christ took him off to glory. Death by sickness is hard to watch – and it has its own terrors and fears as you watch others be chaperones to the one you love – who may not love him <u>at all</u> – or worse, totally despise him.

But before that I had faced death in a less refined version – less slowly, painstakingly version – in its raw, instantaneous form.

Ahh the boxcars – nice, neat little cabins on wheels for a wary traveler – but often when parked in a "big" city, you'd feel like a sitting duck – and violent, often drunken gang men would leer as they walked by – checking for someone who was at least asleep – Sometimes the Lord took care of them directly – Sometimes others did – as in the instruments of wrath, for the Lord. I well remember, the time we paused overnight, in a town in California, perhaps Bakersfield – oh a young guy was sitting by a fire on a cold day and warming his hands – He studies us curiously and invited us over. We chatted amicably, even testified about Jesus to him, but his face showed a coldness as we shared our faith. Yeah he seemed friendly enough – He handed us a little something to eat and we gave him some food we had too, and an extra P-38 can opener that he needed – and we went on our way as it was getting dark – to the long line of stopped boxcars, to get some sleep. We walked about a quarter of a mile down – to a boxcar and rested rather nervously as we watched groups of men walk by – drunk and rowdy. My dear husband – who is quite gifted by the Holy Spirit – suddenly sat up and smiled. He said he saw a big purest white angel of the Lord manifest in light, by the boxcar door, and he knew we would be safe. We fell asleep in our shared sleeping bag in holy comfort at the thought of our angels taking care of us, which sometimes even I would see too, on occasion. Anyway, other men walked by but we knew from experience, the angel of the Lord <u>could</u> blind men to us, when we were in danger.

Next morning – we got up refreshed from our little boxcar sleep – and headed down the tracks about where we met this young guy – only he was gone, and another hobo was making a fire by the bridge overpass area. He was an older guy – very big – typical looking hobo, salt and pepper crew cut graying hair, in his 40s, lots of clothes on, but strong as an ox – a former veteran. He invited us over as well, for some coffee. He mentioned he had some trouble during the night – we mentioned all the rowdy men – suddenly he brought out a thin polished piece of wood, an axe handle – "yes," he said, smacking his hand, "a young guy came across me and tried to roll me last night – but I had my equalizer with me" – Not used to violence, I remember feeling my stomach drop and my husband laughed nervously. "Yes," he continued, "I bashed him in the head – and that took care of him." I felt sick. He mentioned later that they had taken him to the hospital. The railroad workers had called the police... Suddenly, I knew in a flash from the Lord what had happened – I asked for a description of this man – he was the young guy we both had chatted with – I asked where the older veteran had camped that night – in a boxcar right by ours, on a <u>long</u> line – I knew then, that with his thick, broad shoulders, under the covers he had passed for me and John sleeping together – and this young guy who thought we were weak, had watched us and figured out at a distance the approximate boxcar we were at – but the Angel of the Lord had met him, and made him go to the wrong one, and he met this man instead with his equalizer. Then the Lord Jesus spoke this scripture to me clearly – Proverbs 7:11 "an evil man seeks only rebellion; therefore a cruel messenger shall be sent against him." – I felt chills as I thought of how this young guy – who was strong, but no match for this seasoned veteran – well-traveled stocky man, with his quick reaction time and sudden fury – So I knew that God – judged this young man – for trying to roll us – picking on a couple of "holy rollers" who did him no harm, and he thought was a couple of cream puffs. Perhaps he thought we were rich – but we were not… we were penniless as usual, praise the Lord! Most times though, I remember the Lord Jesus came through for us in a "mystical" way when violence came near us – But nonetheless, the Lord Jesus' angel brought confusion on this young guy to meet his judgment. Perhaps God had had enough, of his predatory ways, and wanted him to start thinking about eternity – and where his soul was going to end up. Next time it could be his life. We must know – as Christians who are serving God – that if we are in your Calling, in the United States or Timbuktu – He <u>will</u> protect us one way or another, as long as it's not our time to go and we are where we belong – or are supposed to be – for after all death is our graduation and reward! When it is time! Something to look forward to. Though, I <u>was</u> mad my older husband left before me, and I was left behind – At least, I'm comforted that he is happy ever after in the arms of Jesus, because <u>Jesus never fails</u>… Especially when you die! Whether by murder or execution or natural causes – God will meet the believer on the other side – Heaven! Oh – filled with His Glory and Grace – <u>Heaven is a Beautiful Place</u>!

Chapter 20

THE FIRST TIME JOHN DIED

John was not afraid to die... But he once was afraid of dying and he shared with me how he overcame the fear of death. As a young Christian of 30 years old, he confessed this weakness to the Lord Jesus every night about his fear of death. You see John had been to 14 very dismal funerals by the age of 30. Some were quite orthodox and traditional with prayers for the dead. He told the Lord Jesus every day, "I love you and I fear you Lord Jesus, but please forgive me, I fear death." Those 14 morbid funerals had taken their toll on him – Laying more emphasis on, "praying for the dead," than on a happy graduation. Thus John feared not dying as much as being left in the grave. His own mother and father had died by the time he was 23 years old, in a 3 year time span. So Jesus took care of his fear in a remarkable way. He took John on a trip to Heaven.

John had just been restored to Christ for a year and a half and his dear uncle had just died a few months earlier. John had taken care of this man who was once a big strong steel-mill worker, who had both his legs amputated because of his diabetes. John led him to Christ and watched him happily die and make it to Heaven! He even saw a vision his uncle was in Heaven – just <u>before</u> he died. Meanwhile, John was still overcoming smoking but trying to quit. So he would throw packs of cigarettes away, but still buy some more, (as he smoked five packs a day at that time). Anyway he was saying his prayers one night, and lay down on his couch in his uncle's two-story home. Suddenly he saw a huge black angel of death, with wings and all, walk in the room. It reached its hand out and pointed to John. John rebuked him in the name of Jesus and it still walked towards him. Then he remembered the scriptures in Jude 1:9, how Michael the Archangel dared not rebuke the devil but said instead, "the Lord rebuke you." So John said, "The Lord rebuke you!," however the dart of death still came out as the Dark Angel pointed his hand and it hit John in the chest. Suddenly, he saw two beautiful Angels of the Lord, in purest light. They came down from Heaven. The angel of death immediately left heading downward. The beautiful Angels of the Lord said to my husband John, "you have a fear of death and the Lord Jesus Christ sent us to take you on a trip to Heaven!"

John had both his hands crossed over his chest and he said, "Oh no, no, no, no, no – I don't want to die," as he was shaking his head vehemently. Suddenly, he was in between both Angels standing up. Each Angel put one arm under each of his legs, and a hand under each arm, and <u>up</u> they went through the high 2-story ceiling of his uncle's house. He could feel the wind – suddenly, he looked down and saw his body down below, with his mouth still open, and his arms crossed over his chest! And he said, "Oh my God, I died! I died!"

Well up through the ceiling they went and he even saw his aunts upstairs sleeping in their room. He could see himself, his soul, that looked just like himself and he could "feel" the air (of course that's why we feel pain in Hell and pleasure in Heaven, because our souls have feelings).

As he traveled up and beyond his home he came to a place where wicked spirits in high places dwell. Demons came with chains and screamed racing at him – But lo and behold there was a protective bubble of light around him, as well as his two Angel friends. He was invincible. Next he came to an area as he traveled upward that was <u>total darkness</u>. He couldn't even see himself, not even the angels who were holding him, though they were still there. I always thought that that was the "Valley of the Shadow of Death" that he was going through, as in Psalm 23. Anyway in this dark place he got nervous and thought "maybe they are going to take me on a trip to Hell instead." (Forgetting for an instant that he was told he was going to Heaven.) Suddenly he started acting like the parable of the "Pharisee and the Publican". He said, "Lord, I read my Bible today, 10 chapters, and witnessed in my cab today (he was a cab driver then), and I worshipped you a couple of hours – but there is one thing I have to say, I haven't given up cigarettes, yet – but when I get back in that body, I will." The Angels spoke to him and said, "Calm down Thomas, calm down!" (He later went by his middle name. Thomas was his original first name.) So John arrived and suddenly he saw an entrance made right into the Kingdom of Heaven – (just like the scriptures say – "an entrance shall be made for you") – and he was in the Kingdom of Light – Heaven – He saw a beautiful fountain of water of purest light, and mansions in the distance, also of purest light with souls walking around in the distance. He started dancing around the fountain saying, "I made it; I made it!" He was so happy! Suddenly the Angel of the Lord tapped him on the shoulder. This special Angel of the Lord was in blue silver light. He thought he was the Holy Spirit – and he appeared as a man to him and said to him, "You're going back down." And John slapped his knees and said, "What, I just got here!" The man in silver blue light said to him, "the Lord Jesus brought you up to Heaven because you had a fear of death – Now when death comes your way, you will have joy unspeakable and full of glory – and your life will be threatened many times with guns and knives – and you will have holy joy."

Indeed, he did have a holy joy when his life was threatened with guns and knives even before he met me – and also after when we were together, we would have life threatening experiences – and he had no more fear of death – But that holy joy unspeakable, and full of glory. Praise the Lord Jesus! So John said, "Oh, ok," and the angels took him back down – and he had no fear, and put him in his body – and he noted they put him in his belly ("out of the belly shall flow rivers of living water"). And also after he was in his body, it was sealed up with light all over him – "sealed with the Holy Spirit," as the scriptures say. He watched the angels go up with a wave of the hand, and he suddenly sat up – 45 minutes had passed, he saw on his watch. He was ice cold – he got up and said, "no one will ever believe this happened to me." Then without thinking he lit up a cigarette. "Oh man," he said, "I was going to quit." But God showed him a big blue light, which means "the answer is on its way" – and the size of it indicated about 3 months more before he'd quit. God was teaching him that it was <u>Him</u> who delivered him, in <u>His</u> timing so he would never glory in his flesh, or give people a hard time about smoking.

Then he called up his good cab driving friends, who brought him back to Christ, at 28 years old. His friend David, who he always fellowshipped with, was from a Pentecostal family and his relatives happened to be visiting. So David listened over the phone, and then relayed it to his family, what John had experienced. The Holy Ghost bore witness that he had been to Heaven, and they all started jumping and praising the Lord Jesus, and giving John, "prophesies" for his life.

Next, John, who used to go by his first name "Thomas," was still a doubter then – and asked the Lord Jesus to <u>still</u> prove it happened to him – So he suddenly felt led to go to the laundry-mat and do his clothes. He walked to it and had his laundry going and noticed a little old lady, reading her Bible and he said to her – "Say is that a Christian worker's New Testament Bible?" And she said, "Why yes, son, and I'm saved, baptized, and filled with the Holy Ghost and fire, and I have been caught up to Heaven <u>three</u> times." My husband said, "What? That just happened to me and I'm having a hard time believing it." "Well," she explained, "you know, I had control over saying I was saved and baptized, but I had no control over saying I got caught up to Heaven three times. I didn't even articulate it. I don't go around saying that to perfect strangers – they might throw me into the loony bin." So she got her elderly husband and he showed John three death certificates she had and told him how she one time even died in the hospital and was put in the morgue, and woke up <u>right in the morgue</u>! What a shock to the medical workers! Each time she spent up in Heaven was for many hours and she saw a lot – and was able to comfort many senior citizens about the reality of Heaven. So John was extremely comforted that his experience was real and what a confirmation! And when he was sent out on his dangerous lifestyle of traveling and hitch-hiking a short time later, and later with me freight-train riding, he did not fear death when it came his way many times. At times he even had to keep from laughing when one man held a gun to his head. What a testimony of God's transforming power!

However, John wondered exactly what she meant by the word "articulate" as he had only a 10th grade education because of his ulcerative colitis. So John had a <u>demonstration</u> for himself, a short time later. One time he was out with a pastor friend who took off to get him a Dairy Queen in Pittsburg, PA. Meanwhile John was witnessing to a drugged-out hippie guy who had come up to him. John had his hair very short at the time and looked very bourgeois. He asked this guy if he knew about Jesus. The man became livid and flipped out a switch blade and put the tip right against John's belly, and said, "Are you a Jesus freak?" "Yes," John said, "whatever you want to call me." The man answered, "Then how come you don't have long hair?" and started pushing the knife in John's belly more. John was standing on his toes, trying to avoid the knife by now. The Scripture, 1 Cor. 9:22, came to John and he wanted to say, "I am made all things to all men, that I might by all means save some."

He could feel the pain of the knife and out of his mouth a voice took over, coming right from his belly, as he opened his mouth, and the voice said, "I Am that I Am!" John said, he didn't even articulate, it just came out of his mouth – the man dropped the knife shaking and actually peed his pants and in a shaking voice said, "Yeah, yeah, yeah," and took off running. And then the "pastor friend" came quickly over, with two Dairy Queens, and saw the guy taking off. He picked up the knife and said, "What happened here?" And John told him how the great "I Am" Ex. 3:14, Jn.8:58, had spoken through him, and how he saw the Holy Ghost purest blue silver light all over him when the Holy Ghost spoke through him. The pastor said, "We'll just have to have you tell that testimony in church this morning, brother, because the Holy Ghost really <u>bears witness</u> through you! Jn. 8:18/ And so he did that very morning! And many souls were refreshed about the way God can divinely intervene when you are up against the wall – (or a switchblade, ha, ha!)

And John really understood what the little old lady at the laundry-mat had meant, when she said, "I didn't even articulate the last part about being caught up to Heaven 3 times!"

By the way... John didn't stop smoking the minute he got back in his body – he almost immediately lit up another cigarette, but he <u>did</u> see a bluish light meaning "answers on the way" for the time it would take to quit, which by the size, (size had to do with time) it looked 3 months. And it was 3 months exactly. And when the blue light he saw was the size of a dot and he said "get me behind Satan" this time, and he was able to quit for the rest of his life! All together it had taken him a year and a half to break his 5 packs of cigarettes a day that he had begun at 15 years old, and was now 30 years old. Because it was a slow deliverance, Jesus taught him by that, never to be hard on people struggling with their various habits and that the deliverance didn't come from mere self-control but from the Lord Jesus Christ! And amazingly, the doctors had told him his lungs were all black and within just a short time after he quit, his lungs were totally cleared up, the doctor said, which is highly unlikely. It was a miracle!

Chapter 21

The Healing Journey

When we travel by freight train we often landed in Colton, California – a regular hobo junction and a pretty good place to rest – plenty of box cars in the yards that weren't going anywhere for a while. Anyway, we first went to McDonalds after a long freight ride and met another traveler named Harold who shared his personal history, and we got to talk and pray with him – he had broken his ribs in a recent altercation and nothing seemed to help him, not even prayers from a local church that he attended that we knew to be somewhat anti-homeless. Since nothing seemed to subdue the pain, John and I felt led to pray for him for a healing. We did, and he thanked us, and immediately felt better! We fellowshipped a couple of hours and then went on our way. When we parted, me and John slept in the same boxcar by the railroad tracks that we had slept in the night before. We met a man on the boxcar when we woke up in the morning. He had got in much later and had slept on the other end and had been drinking a lot. In the morning he was standing toward the middle of the boxcar coughing heavily, really suffering withdrawals from the night before. He was scared. We asked him if we could pray for him and he didn't want to be touched because of his culture. He was an Indian chief from Canada and a very tall man with long hair. But he thanked us and did want prayer. He felt better and we spent a few days with this man, Larry, who had a really sore back, too. So we offered to pray for that, too, but he was unsure, so we didn't want to push him until he had <u>more</u> faith.

He was thinking about it a couple of days when we went to McDonalds in the evening and shared a large coffee together. And lo and behold, as we sat there, there was Harold, the homeless man whose ribs we had prayed for. He had a couple beers and was very uninhibited and he spoke openly to us and Larry with joyful abandon. Loudly – he said, "Hey" pointing to us, "there's those two people who healed my ribs," he told Larry. He pointed at us and his face flushed, as he said loudly again, "Jesus healed me through their prayers," and he grabbed his ribs, "I have no pain, after I suffered for weeks. Jesus healed me." (Even the pastor's prayers of a local church hadn't healed him.) Well, the Lord Jesus sure used Harold to help us concerning Larry. Larry was quite impressed and after our coffee, he and John and I, headed to a boxcar and he asked us to pray for him and we did. We prayed for the Lord Jesus to heal his back. He was healed – he said it felt great.

And the next morning we walked down with him, Larry-Victory we called him because we knew another Larry, and Larry means victory (or laurel, like a victor's wreath). We headed to the freights with him as he was parting to head to Yuma, Arizona, and we still felt led to head back to Colton and go the opposite way. So we said our goodbyes beside the grain car he picked to ride. The train he was on was all set up to be going soon, engines and all. And he thanked John for reminding him to be thankful and he said he knew the Lord Jesus. (But in his Indian ways he always used to be thankful, he said.) John would always openly praise and thanks the Lord for everything – So Larry thanked him for reminding him to be thankful again! And we parted – happily, Larry with a healed back, and me and John marveling at how Jesus had used us for two healings that month with Larry and Harold. What joy and sweet victory we felt as we walked back to Colton – looking like the scum of the earth to most people, but feeling like Kings – Kings of the Road!

Chapter 22

AIRBAGS-FEARS

When we journey for the Lord Jesus we weren't always snow-birds, as they say on the freight trains. That means when the weather gets cold, you head south. But because we were on a divine mission we traveled wherever the Holy Spirit led us, and it didn't always happen to be warm places. Why we traveled right through Glacier National Park, in the wintertime in Montana, on a piggy-back, <u>on</u> the high-line, <u>at</u> <u>night</u>!

When you catch a train out of Spokane, Washington – you have a choice of a high-line or a low-line route. As we learned the first time from some brakemen, working in Spokane yards – the low-line takes you from Spokane, WA., to Sandypoint, Idaho – and then veers towards Missoula, Montana, Helena, MO, and eventually Laurel, MO. The high-line takes you from Spokane WA. to also Sandypoint, ID, and veers up to the high-line to Whitefish, MO, then to Havre, MO and eventually you land in the Anoka yards of Minnesota

Anyway, it was exciting! But how did we ever survive the bitter cold. The wind-chill factor alone can decrease the temperature 40 degrees colder when you're going 30-50 miles an hour. The answer – is "Airbags" – that's how! An old hobo trick we learned from fellow tramps that saved us many a time – we'd find old discarded airbags often in empty boxcars. They were used on a shipment of merchandise that they didn't want to shift to injure the cargo. So they would put these airbags in between different sections of the merchandise. So anyway, me and John found an old boxcar with a left over airbag and, as we were told, we ripped off the brown paper which revealed a plastic airbag – it was wide enough for the <u>both</u> of us to sleep in, and so we sliced it open on top and put our one sleeping bag over our feet like a quilt laying on top of our tarp and rubber mat, then slipped the airbag over our sleeping bag and all. We used the sleeping bag over us as a quilt to get more body heat. Anyway, we rode over the mountains of Glacier National Park, in the wintertime at night, on a piggyback, which is pretty open as we were on a flat car with a truck trailer on top, and our windbreak is only the huge wheels of the trailer, which is chained to the flat car. So that's how it was – oh we precipitated a lot under that thick plastic airbag, but it kept us nice and warm, so we could enjoy the sparkling beautiful white snow of Glacier National Park, in the wintertime, at night. I thought I was in Heaven, except for the cold, as we were winding slowly through the snowy mountainous landscape and pine trees.

So now that I told you all that, I'll tell you how the Lord Jesus delivered me from the <u>fear of cold</u>! My husband John – he was from Pittsburgh, Pennsylvania – so he had a good tolerance for cold, having experienced snowy winters and all… I got that expression from John, saying "and all" at the end of a sentence. That's a very Pittsburghian thing to say or "n that"… and also, "you all" was always yo'uns – which I thought was so very cute.

Anyway, my upbringing was in good 'ole California, Southern yet, in Los Angeles County. So I was pretty used to warm weather. The first time I left California with my husband – in our first year of traveling – I was pretty sure of myself with 100% wool sweater and corduroy pants and a pea coat. I had a little '63 VW bug, a college graduation 1976 gift from my Dad. We first traveled in it and I was sure I would be plenty warm. My husband wisely bought me a knit hat, a pretty rose pink beret I'll never forget. It was June – nice weather 'til we headed across the states to visit his relatives, and suddenly one night we were sleeping in our car by a rest stop in New Mexico, and the temperature dropped and a cold wind blew that cut right through my wool sweater and pea coat and I couldn't believe it. I was freezing. So that was the beginning of cold weather 101 for me, the naïve native Californian (after that I learned the wonders of <u>long underwear</u>!)

So the next big test came a few years later in a freight train ride when I was with my buddy John, a more seasoned traveler now, we had had to part with our car after putting 90,000 miles on it traveling all over the USA, and hitch-hiked a year or so as well and took a year off to rest in Sacramento after a job injury where Jesus led us into the freight train experience together for the <u>first time</u>. John had hitch-hiked seven years for Jesus before he met me but he had never ridden the freight trains. We learned that together!

Anyway – we were in Dalhart, Texas and we knew the Lord Jesus wanted us to head over the Colorado Mountains into Denver. We waited in the yards for hours in chilly weather – this was wintertime mind you – and the only freight trains that came through finally were coal cars that were empty so we got a nice coal car ride. Beside getting sooty, these coal cars had one drawback – some coal cars are built with a slowly slanting wall you can walk down into (these are empties remember), so they have little indentations for steps – but these coal cars were almost straight up with very little incline and pretty steep – so you walk up the ladder on the outside and drop into it, but you couldn't just walk out of it – John, of course, being a gentleman that he was climbed the ladder first and sat on top and helped me drop down after I climbed the ladder, as I was only 5'2" – John was 5'11" – but the trick was getting out. So we got in our sleeping bag and our sliced open air bag around us, pondering the steep incline and talking about ways to get out. We laid down on this cold metal floor, surrounded by metal that seemed so difficult to get out, especially in freezing weather, in a metal pit! John held me very close, but despite his body heat and the air bag – as we climbed over the steep Colorado Mountains at night, and it was getting colder by the second – I got scared! I kept thinking how we were trapped in that steel coal car and could feel the cold, numb my fingers and burn them. As I was creeping through the winding mountain pass, my mind had fantasies of freezing to death in a cold metal car, unnoticed – and tears of fright from the burning cold came to my eyes. It was too noisy to talk to John in the noisy coal car lumbering through the mountains. I cried out to Jesus to protect us – and as you know, fear always makes things worse. Suddenly, as I was praying I had a vision. I saw a <u>huge</u> wave coming at me like it would drown me – then suddenly, the wave disappeared, and it became a little trickle of water on the ground, and I walked right over it! And the Holy Spirit said to me in a still small voice, "That's your Fear and you're going to be alright" – and he was right. Coming from Southern California the cold was a shock to me, unlike John who was from Pittsburgh, PA! And so the large wave became a trickle!

We arrived in Denver at about 5 in the morning – the sun was shining – it was a warm 0 degrees, I remember seeing on the temperature sign when we came in. With the wind chill factor on the train we were probably suffering about minus 25 degrees, so zero degrees felt warm. We stopped in the yards and John figured out how to get us out of there. First, I got on his back and stood on him to tie a cord we had to the top of the ladder. Then John got our packs in a pile, tied the cord to the packs and stood on the packs to heist himself on top of the ledge, balancing himself there. My arms weren't as strong so I couldn't heist myself all the way up. So as I stood on the backpacks he pulled me up by the arms and then I was sitting on the ledge with John, and I felt like my arms had grown a few inches as he had pulled me up. As we sat up there, we pulled up the two packs to the top, and slowly lowered them down to the other side. Then we crawled down the "outside" ladder, merrily chatting at our great escape. Praise the Lord Jesus! He always came through! And I overcame my fear of the cold once and for all! What an acrobatic feat that was! We headed down happily to a free coffee place – a little hang out for the homeless or tramps like us, and enjoyed the rest of our day in Denver – the mile high city.

An Angelic Experience in Denver, Colorado

While we were in Colorado, I want to tell you of the Great and Mighty God's Marvelous protection. Me and John landed in Denver numerous times in our freight train travels, and it was hard to always find a sleeping spot – Oh, there were obvious places along the canal, where numerous tramps slept and even the city folk could see the tents out in the open, but we didn't like to be where there were lots of people. My dear husband always liked to hide me well – he knew what "evil lurked in the hearts of men" and he would call me his "little diadem".

So we found a pretty good spot, in a lowly residential area, that had a huge field that was lined with thick trees – perfect hiding places for wayfarers – though it wasn't the safest neighborhood – we decided to stay by the edge of the field. We were completely out of water and dehydrated so rather than send me out in the late evening, John left me on the edge of the field waiting with the backpacks while he went searching for water – heading down a little street and disappearing. Across the street from me was a rowdy liquor store and I was getting nervous as I saw a bad element lingering by the liquor store.

Anyway, I was feeling rather vulnerable and praying for protection when lo and behold God opened up my eyes and I saw a big Angel of the Lord manifest. He was at least 10 feet tall, purest white, with wings and all. And he looked quite able to protect me. I felt his love and security immediately. Probably one of my angels that regularly protected me, no doubt. I praised the Lord Jesus as I felt his marvelous peace descend upon me, and John who had to go to several houses to find water, came back a half hour or more later, reappearing with a gallon canteen full of water from a local neighbor. And of course I shared with John my wonderful experience of seeing an Angel of the Lord protecting me and he nodded joyfully as he had seen many angels in his longer journeys, than I had – plus he even saw Holy Ghost purest blue-silver light on what I <u>said</u> about my angelic encounter!

Chapter 23

A Miracle in Indiana

We came to a town somewhere in Indiana one day and I had a vision – my tennis shoes were on me and the shoes turned into hiking boots, then I heard "more power, more persecution". And the vision ended. So I discerned the Holy Spirit saying he was going to bring me into more power, and the bigger shoes represented this power, and also it would come with "more persecution".

Ironically, that day a saintly soul blessed us with $20 or so and my dear John, seeing winter was coming, bought me a pair of hiking boots with that blessing, and I tossed my sneakers out. But I still knew the vision related to a spiritual happening and God was graphically showing me.

So we were lead up to a church and determined to attend it Sunday morning. During the night, as we rested in the bushes, I suddenly started to pray intercessory prayer, and I didn't even know what for (as I was praying in tongues), but the power of God was on me so strong I easily prayed from 12 midnight to 5 in the morning nonstop. We got up from our little sleeping spot around 7 and headed towards this church to arrive at the 9am service. I told John how I was up all night long praying and even had a vision of an overflowing pot of coffee, like God was keeping me awake. Well, we walked into what was obviously a Pentecostal church, looking like a couple of seedy, worn-out travelers with our dusty clothes and well worn out backpacks, and we found a seat, and sat down. It was lots of loud music with a band for worship and a little woman with a big voice burst out in song. Then the Pastor, who was a woman, was in distress, asking for prayers from anyone, for a spiritual problem she couldn't identify. So numerous people went up to lay hands on her but nothing seemed to relieve her anguish. Suddenly, the Spirit of the Lord came on me, and I knew I had a prophecy for her. I thought, I can't just go up there – she doesn't even know me – blah blah blah! I whispered to John that I had a prophecy and he encouraged me as he saw purest light over me. As I saw people file back to their seats and her still upset and crying out to Jesus – I got my courage up and went to give her the prophesy. It was a blockbuster though I didn't expect it to be – the word of the Lord simply was, that "you have treated your Heavenly Father like your earthly father and because your earthly father had ridiculed and mocked you (as an alcoholic) and even scared you as a child, the Heavenly Father says how much He loves you and is not like this, and loves you with tender love." Well I had my hand outstretched, but not touching her at all, and suddenly she fell backward as I spoke, like being slain in the Spirit. I was shocked as that had never happened to me before. They caught her and she continued to hear me out as I finished the prophecy. Suddenly a young man in the back of the small church leaped up and said loudly, "I've been healed!" It turned out, as the anointing fell for the prophecy, a deaf young man, who even had a surgical implant in his ear, suddenly was <u>healed miraculously</u> and could hear perfectly and he leapt up for joy. And they even told me that he (later) donated $100 to the church for the miracle he had received. So I went back to my seat, rather astounded myself, and realized this was "more power" I stayed up all night for praying – the "bigger shoes". And the pastor's daughter, the young woman that sang, asked us over to her house and we spent nine days fellowshipping with her and her husband.

During that time of fellowship with this young woman, a lot of healing took place and personal things got revealed. As me and my husband were intercessors and we prayed for this young woman to be set free of some abusive history she had gone through and never confessed and it instantly healed her of physical as well as emotional problems. She had kept these skeletons in the closet for a long time and she was feeling really good – so good she called up the offending family members involved – and told them off – And they wanted to kill us. Well one of the guiltiest members came up with a great idea, and he even told our young friend his scheme on the telephone. He was going to trump up a charge against us strangers and we'd be in jail in no time. He, one of her previous abusers, actually told her that, as he was very threatened about his reputation in the church. She hung up the phone and told us the threat and said naively, "I'll visit you in jail!" And that's when John and I looked at each other and got alone and yes, we felt the Holy Ghost saying "it's not my will for you to go to jail for these liars – Go!" And so we said goodbye to the young woman and her husband and off we went – "When they persecute you in this city, flee ye to another," Matt.10:23! There it was, the "more persecution" that came with "more power", as my vision had revealed previously.

Two weeks had passed and we were glad to be off again... On The Road Again! Backpacks and all. We were blessed with $10 by our young friend who was delivered and happier, and with that we headed down the tracks and had some coffee and some good praying time after that "circus city". Jesus rescued us from the mouth of the lion once again.

Chapter 24

Turn Around

"Foxes and holes, and birds of the air have nests; but the Son of man (and his disciples, John always said) hath not where to lay his head." Mt.8:20

You have to have a tender conscience when you live outside – you never know who will walk up on you – For a Christian it is a great discipline – you really learn how to pray... and pray we did – every morning, every night, throughout the day... And you never know when traveling, <u>where</u> you would "lay your head to rest." – Oh we might slow down somewhere and find a good spot for awhile, but only as long as the Lord Jesus gave us peace – and sometimes it was intruders that moved us along – or well meaning do-gooders that called the cops on us – But because we were in the Lord's will and Calling – for the most part we had favor in our incognito lifestyle that people and cops were either blind or kind. We used to, in fact, ask the Lord (and I still do) to blind cops and people who would want to bother us, or that they would be blind or kind. And He did! How did we know? Well, we were in Kansas City, Kansas, one of many times. We'd come out by the Missouri River there by the railroad tracks where we had arrived by freight train and we'd go back and forth into town to check the dumpsters for food – go to the library for rest, and go back to the railroad tracks and cook some food we'd found, down by the riverside. That was our little routine.

One time when we were foraging for food – we ran into another couple of transients and they told us how in <u>this town</u> the cops always bothered you and they had a hard time there <u>every</u> time. They said, "We had to lay low and we weren't doing anything suspicious, just 'homeless,' – they'd threaten us and move us along with unreasonable harassment!" These tramps were just picking through the trash for discarded scrap metal to turn in for money. Usually when tramps are doing this, they are pretty much on the honest side. So, anyway, we had been through this town a number of times and had never been bothered by the cops. They must be blind to us, we thought, God honored our prayer. This may have been at least the third time we were in this area by the river, so we left peaceably as usually undetected. Jesus sent us there again about a year later and we had always noticed the only time cops were "allowed" to bother us was when we were not getting the directions right – from the Lord Jesus. After all cops, though not <u>all</u> on the good side, are ministers of the law and if we were doing good for the Lord Jesus, He would use them to reroute us when we were misguided, otherwise He'd blind them to us. So sure enough, this time John was getting a check on riding the freight trains, somewhat sensing to hitch-hike instead. Well, John had hitch-hiked for <u>7</u> years straight on his own, and about 2 years with me, and he much preferred his new mode of travel via "freight train express"! – Unbeknownst to me, as we entered the town, John pretty clearly <u>had</u> gotten from the Lord to hitch-hike, but he had decided to resist, hoping the impression would <u>go away</u>. There we were blithely sitting in the library and there were <u>5 minutes</u> to spare before closing time – We were tired warriors of the road, and were trying to gather our stuff to leave, and in walked 2 cops into this little library – as if we were wanted criminals they said, "the library is closing" – "We know," we said and we pointed to the clock with 5 minutes to spare, "that's why we're gathering out stuff." "Oh well, you need to move along" – and then they actually checked our ID in the library and off they went! Amazingly as we were walking down towards the street, some other cops bothered us. "Are you going to the railroad tracks" they asked us. "No," John said. "Well that's good," they said, "don't go there," and off they went. After they left, I looked at John shocked, who didn't have a habit of lying, and I said, "Well aren't we going to go try to catch a freight train dear?" I asked. Well then he told me how God was dealing with him to hitch-hike instead and he was avoiding it. And he knew that's why the cops had bothered him twice by then. So like a good warrior for the Lord Jesus, John admitted his error and made it right, bravely heading to the highway, where we walked and then hitch-hiked for a while.

We got a ride that night, around 10pm, and had amazing fellowship with a young man who took us to his home to testify to his family who were Christians. We were used there for a healing of a woman who had some diabetic problems. The woman was so thrilled that she boasted to her pastor on the telephone and Jesus also used us in her local church to set her elderly pastor free of an awful persecution he'd endured from false prophets in his church who tried to take his church over by force.

So you see, it was a God-ordained ride! Jesus had a plan for us to hitch-hike and he used 2 officers as ministers of the law, to re-guide us – ha ha! We were no longer invisible when we got out from the "covering of the Lord," briefly heading in the wrong direction. The freight trains would have headed us in the wrong direction and we would have been miserable indeed with unfinished business. Even with ornery cops who just like to pick on transients for no good reason – God can blind them to you if you're in God's will – because "when a man's ways please the Lord, he makes even his enemies to be at peace with him." Pr. 16:7

At any rate, we were at peace in "Policeville" when we got on track! Or rather on the road again, in this case!

I must mention, on this trip to Osatoame, Kansas, the Holy Spirit taught us an important prayer. Like I said, when the dear woman who was healed boasted to her pastor of a Charismatic church of her healing, he wanted to meet us the next day. So we started walking down to the church, which wasn't too far, to meet this elderly pastor who was about 70 years old. He probably was a pastor for about 50 years. We were all jubilant as we walked, expecting some great applause, but instead as we were walking along, the Holy Spirit dealt with us and told us this man does not want to pat you on the back. He <u>already</u> has something against you and will try to interrogate you. So the Holy Spirit told us to pray, (out loud), an accountability prayer he had taught us previously.

So we arrived in a church room and he started to chat with us and ask us questions. We could feel the tension in the air. My husband stopped him and said politely, "Would you mind if we prayed a prayer first." "Sure," he said. So John prayed, "Father in Heaven, hold us accountable to the Kingdom of God in this man and hold him accountable to the Kingdom of Heaven in us, and have us be one in the Spirit, in Jesus' name." As soon as we prayed that, he started talking in a different way. God turned the tables around and instead of him questioning us, he became very cheerful and told us how he had rode the freight trains as a young guy, and being 70 year old, he did it when it was very difficult (very mean railroad bulls – think Ernest Borgnine movie!). And we ended up having wonderful fellowship, and he shared more about himself. He was so relaxed. As we stood up to leave, he finally shared the secret of his heart that could have caused us contention, he said "when I heard you two were prophets, I had it in for you," he confessed, "two false prophets had come to my church, and we allow prophesy here, but they had stood up to say that God sent them to replace me, and that I needed to leave. I was devastated and even thought of leaving, but my friends told me not to buckle and that these people were not of the Lord. So I had it in for you, when I heard you all were prophets too, and was going to put you thru the grill, but I see that God has "good" prophets too, and I am blessed." And we prayed that he would be healed of the trauma in Jesus' name, and he rejoiced! We thanked Jesus, he was so refreshed! And so were we! And that was the final crescendo of our hitch-hiking detour to Osatoame, Kansas. A pastor was restored, after being traumatized by "wolves in sheep's clothing." Hallelujah!

Chapter 25

JUDGMENT BEGINS AT THE HOUSE OF GOD

"Judgment must begin at the house of God" 1 Peter 4:17-18 – Judgment is a big deal in Christendom – but it is often misunderstood. I've heard some preachers actually preach that you can't judge and leave it there – Oh very well then let's go follow former cult leader Jim Jones and not judge him – he claimed to be born again and did good deeds – we'll just <u>not</u> judge him on the fact that he was perverse and sick. Many people followed him and ended up dead – We, by God's permission, are of course <u>allowed</u> to judge. How else would we be able to judge the <u>wolves</u> in sheep's clothing – And figure out their fruits are bad – "ye shall know them by their fruits!" Matthew 7:15-21. It's like cutting off your hands, to say,-you can't judge- as a blatant statement. To <u>survive</u> we need sound judgment – knowing the word of God, and discerning a person by the <u>Holy Spirit</u> – and, of course, living a holy life ourselves helps to sharpen our discernment immensely. For instance, the famous Romans 2:1-11 scripture speaks of not judging – but if you read on, the rebuke is obvious. Twice it speaks of not judging another person if <u>you</u> yourself are guilty of the same sin. If you steal, don't judge someone else who is stealing. Don't act high and mighty if you have the same sin. This is pharisaic plain and simple. I always liked the example of some of those preachers on TV, who would say, "don't give to bums on the street, but give to me!" and yet they were themselves "glorified panhandlers". How hypocritical! The man on the street might just need a few bucks to survive – it's true, he or she might have some bad vices or habits, or be a little greedy in some areas – there are, of course, outright scammers on the street, too! But how much more someone who is using God's people as a means to pay for their show-offy <u>fancy</u> cars and mansions and very expensive habits – how about <u>that</u> for panhandling – that is "making merchandise out of God's people", 2 Pe.2:3. They often say it's for God, but what happened to, Mt. 10:8 "freely you have received and freely you will give"? Sure, a (spiritual) laborer *is* worthy of his (or her) hire, Luke 10:7, but God wants us to be <u>cheerful</u> givers, 2 Cor. 9:7 and not to be extorted by others. A minister that needs to beg for money is a "glorified pan-handler", and there isn't much glory in that – just vain glory. So there you have it in a nut-shell! Wrong judgment – he sees a splinter in a little guy's eye – and he's got a big log of greed in his own face…Matthew 7:1-6. It's an attitude and it's called pride or ego. Famous old-time preachers like Rees Howells never asked for a penny for their ministries, but through prayer, God provided every step of the way – and that's how the Lord Jesus taught John and I to be too, "that our conversation would be without covetousness; and be content with such things as ye have: for He hath said, I will never leave thee, nor forsake thee. So that we can boldly say that the Lord is my helper, and I will not fear what man can do unto me." Hebrews 13:5-6

Next we have another kind of mistake in judgment – and that is outward judgment. We on the road know that lesson well – the lesson of the outward appearance. God's word says, man judges by <u>outward appearance</u>, but God judges by the heart. So we must discern one another's hearts (1 Samuel 16:7) – Can it be done? Yes, by the Holy Spirit through prayer. That's why the Bible says – <u>judge righteous judgment</u>. St. John 7:24. Yes, it really does say <u>we</u> <u>can</u> <u>judge</u>! But in righteous judgment – if we are full of sin, and evil thoughts are in us, watch out we may be committing the classic psychological error of jumping on someone else because we hate the sin <u>in ourselves</u>. We've all seen it and most of us have done it from time to time. It's really a form of self-hatred but it's aiming your gun at a safer target. Thus you have the elite drinker I observed in an outdoor cafe, having a cocktail and looking with utter relish and malice at the stumbling alcoholic with a bottle in his hand and old worn out clothes – and the high class drunkard yells, "get a job you bum" and laughs at his miserable state, while his wife and children blush nervously, tapping his shoulder while he drinks one too many martinis. Secretly he fears he will end up that way – he might, so he picks on an easy target. That's why it says God is a judger of our evil thoughts. He sees past man's well-dressed veneer and God may well give money to that drunk on the street, over this pride-filled man who has no mercy. C.S. Lewis put it well in his book, <u>Mere Christianity</u>, about how "God weighs the spirits". That means God looks deeper into what's really going on – Aren't you glad He does? He sees what caused that man on the street to stumble and what is going on in his heart. He sees the fearful wimp in the sidewalk cocktail drinker and taunter, and how he's too proud to admit his secret fears to God and to cry to God for help... God weighs the spirits and judges people accordingly. Proverbs 16:2

He sees a person's iniquitous sins – what drives them – one person may come from a long line of sinners – they have more to overcome – God sees that. To another person it is easier not to over-drink or to sin in other ways. There were a lot of Christians in their background, but they do it anyway, just for fun – so He judges them accordingly and has mercy accordingly. He looks at the whole picture before he judges that soul.

And remember – the outward appearance is the most convenient excuse to judge or scapegoat people, but the inward appearance is the hardest to discern – that's why Jesus called the Pharisees whited sepulchers (Matthew 23:23-34) – because outwardly they had polished cups, but inwardly they were full of dead men's bones – Jesus rebukes the Pharisees as "snakes" – what a judgment he made because "they loved the praise of men more than the praise of God." John 12:43 So it goes – one man's trash is another man's treasure – and sometimes even "God's treasure" as well! Mt. 6:20-21.

So God looks at the heart – man at the outward appearance, and even though outward appearance may help you discern someone – <u>sometimes</u> – that's why actors transform themselves into characters outwardly first, and yet, it's still only <u>one</u> indicator and may be wrong. As the saying goes, looks can be deceiving so "judge righteous judgment"! And if you can't figure out somebody by inner discernment or don't trust yourself – pray first <u>please</u>. An example of this was a Baptist pastor we met in a Midwest tour when we got off the Illinois Central Golf freight train. The Lord Jesus <u>told</u> us to go to this church!–Because of our appearance we didn't <u>just</u> go to any church, because we never knew the reactions we might get. My husband said to this pastor, "may we worship at this church today?" It was a Sunday evening service. This pastor took one look at us with our big backpacks and our slightly raggedy clothes and he said to us, "Why are you on the road?" And we replied, "we were called to the road and riding the freight trains, by the Lord Jesus Christ." Then he said to us, "Let me pray about you two. I'm going into my office to pray to the Heavenly Father." And sure enough he did. No one was there yet so we just sat there in the pews waiting patiently. Fifteen minutes later he came back and shook our hands and told us we were welcome there. Then, amazingly, during the service he stood up and said, "A couple of travelers have come to my church who rode the freight trains in. I grew up in a military family and looking at them I didn't know what to think, but I prayed to the Heavenly Father, and the Holy Ghost bore witness of them that they are an authentic ministry in the Lord Jesus. So give them the right hand of fellowship when you leave." We didn't know what this meant, but we were happy and then as the service was drawing to a close, each person shook our hand and some people even blessed us, and when we left this church we had $40, enough for bus fare to the next town, and then some. Praise the Lord we were happy! So never judge by outward appearance alone, as this dear pastor stopped himself and had the wisdom to pray first, and God can always surprise us with His answers.

Chapter 26

The Blinding Power of God

The Fox Experience! – My husband John first encountered the blinding power of God when he traveled alone for seven years. He was a young prophet on the road for Jesus and Jesus sent him to an unusual church in Atwater, CA to intercede. He was staying with some Christians and feeling very burdened by the negative element in their assembly from corrupt leaders, although the Christians he was with were very dedicated to Jesus. So he went out into the fields to pray. As he was praying in the Spirit, he had an unusual mystical experience. John had been blessed since he was 12 years old with the gift of discerning of spirits, after he got saved and baptized in the Holy Spirit. He could see things in the spiritual realm if God so let him. He was walking through the fields and praying for a couple of hours and feeling really good and he saw a red fox approach him. The fox didn't even seem to see him, (and they are usually very illusive). The full grown fox walked up to John like a friendly puppy. He was so close that John thought to himself, "I could pat him on the head, but he might bite me." So instead he put his hand out flat and said, "hello mister red fox. And then the fox, with a shocked look, scampered off leaving a trail of dust, and was so startled that it ran into a blackberry bush in its terror. John wondered what had happened, suddenly a few minutes later the fox crept out again cautiously, again he appeared not to see John, only this time God opened up John's eyes. John saw a huge angel of the Lord manifest in front of the fox. The fox grew closer, not seeing John at all. The angel of the Lord was blinding "the fox" to seeing John.

Then John watched this beautiful angel of purest light that was standing in front of the red fox, suddenly step to the right so the fox was exposed. The fox was shocked again and scampered off into the bushes because he could see John. Then the Holy Spirit spoke to John and said, "This red fox represents the leaders that are corrupt in this church. They are foxes, crafty in their nature and they are blinded to who you are, but when I open up their eyes then they will run from you. So in conclusion, John who the corrupt leaders looked at as a traveling bum, eventually was used to speak some heavy truths in his prophetic calling. The people he was staying with were so alarmed at the leaders for persecuting John for speaking the truth of the Bible that they left the church and started their own church that was <u>pure and without corruption</u>. So I told you all this to demonstrate how God can blind people to you when he wants to, with the angel of the Lord. Psalm 91

So anyway, that was John's first blinding testimony and by this God also showed him how some unsafe souls who had ecclesiastical authority did not recognize his Christian walk because they were foxes – or wise in their own conceit, crafty – like Jesus said of Herod – "Go tell that fox", etc. that they could not see the anointing in John's life until the angel of the Lord stepped out of the way – and then spoke through John with power. And suddenly the person (the fox) who gave him a hard time, eyes were opened to see who he was in Christ, and that person took off and ceased to trouble him.

So we who are in Christ must always remember, when some people can't see Christ, the anointing in our "holy" lives, that others see – it may be, they are foxes – and God is allowing them to be blinded – taking them in their own craftiness, until one day He'll suddenly tell the angel of the Lord, to step aside and they'll feel the power of God speak through you, and their eyes will be opened... Do you know any foxes?

Speaking of foxes, years ago when John was going forth in holy boldness as a young Christian and giving out tracts, he decided to just give one to a hostile young man he saw by the bus stop in Pittsburg, Pennsylvania – he said, "here you go young man, Jesus loves you." The young man took the tract and tore it up. "I hate Christians like you," he said "why don't you just give us cigarettes and candy like the mission – but you're into this Holy Ghost and witnessing stuff." Fortunately,

(John thought), the bus came, and he was relieved to see it. As John got on the bus he was dismayed to see the young man get on it too. He sat right near John so that John could observe him. Suddenly he picked up this young man's thought by discernment of the Holy Spirit. He was wanting to cut John's face with a razor, John perceived, and John started praying. Then the young man spoke up, glaring menacingly at John – sure enough, he pulled out a razor for John to see, that was used for slicing open boxes, and said "I'd like to cut your face with this razor but something is stopping me. I just can't do it." John saw silver blue anointing all over himself and touching the young man, and had to keep himself from laughing, as he knew that that was the Holy Spirit stopping the young man from being violent.

So that is how God's Spirit can protect you when you yield to holy boldness and it seems to backfire on you – but as the saying goes, "to be enraged is to be engaged", and so this young man was getting close to the Kindgom of God! At least he knew what he hated – that's why Jesus says, "I'd rather you be hot or cold than luke warm. In his hatred, he found out there was an invisible presence from the God he denied was real!

For instance, just as I shared the experience of how the police were blinded to us when we were doing the right thing in Kansas City, Kansas, that included railroad police as well. Not all "bulls" minded if we rode the freight trains, but there were the few that thought they were Wyatt Earp and would tell us not to ride their train. As for the engineers and brakemen and conductors, they usually were friendly as they didn't mind human cargo. The bull would police them too and always be checking them for drugs, etc. so they enjoyed outfoxing the bull and giving tramps a ride – (except for the Santa Fe lines that were threatened with the loss of their job, if they allowed tramps to ride their trains, so we never rode that train.)(Though one friendly Santa Fe trainman told us we could ride his train if we wanted to, but we didn't.)

John and I were in Spokane, Washington one time and we were heading to Missoula, Montana on the low-line. When we got there we had been warned by other tramps about an especially ornery bull and had managed to avoid him before. This time, however, we got off the train and had actually walked out of the yards, though walking down a little side track by a factory, feeling perfectly safe. Then this nervy Bull starts harassing us about trespassing on railroad property and saying, "don't ride my train" and complaining to John, "why do you have that young woman riding the trains?" John said, "She's my wife and we ride the trains for the Lord Jesus Christ." Well he really blew his top at that and he threatened us some more, but he couldn't do anything because he <u>hadn't</u> caught us on the trains and we really weren't on railroad property. So we spent a few days in that town and the Lord Jesus used us in a local mission feed, and with a few souls we met in a fast food joint who were also transient.

We came back to the yards at night and saw a train all ready to go so we felt inspired to get in the boxcar and even asked God to "blind" the railroad police. Along comes the same guy, who was a real old stickler Bull, and went from boxcar to boxcar shining his beaming light. Then it happened–He came up on us. John said to me, "I guess we're going to jail." So he looked in our car and we were at the end with our bedding all laid out ready to go – he glared his light at us and had a strange blank look on his face, like a deer caught in the headlights, but we were very quiet – and on he headed to the next car. He was blinded by the brighter Light of the Lord Jesus. Hallelujah! I'll never forget that man and we met him a few times more, but he never caught us in a boxcar again. He was always ornery, but we never forgot how God did that! Hallelujah!

Another time in Los Angeles, we were warned of a railroad bull who was terrorizing transients left and right – taking away even their weapons that were <u>closed knives</u> and not returning them. So we heard this warning over and over to watch out for the Bull in L.A. Well, one time we were catching out in the L.A. yards in broad daylight. There was the Bull walking through the yards, looking into each boxcar and we were in one of them. I actually saw, God opened up my spiritual eyes this time, a beautiful turquoise blue light that the Lord Jesus called the blinding angel of the Lord, right in front of the Bull's car. At the same time, Jesus was telling John that he was blinding this Bull in broad daylight. Sure enough, he didn't see us and we had no problem. This happened enough so that we knew it was a real "sign and wonder" that we called it the "Blinding Angel of the Lord". Our train took off a half hour later and we ended up in Yermo, California, and later Las Vegas and Salt Lake City, Utah.

So it got proved to us even further in Hastings, Nebraska, with some middle class folks we met in a Methodist church. We stayed with these missionaries and shared our testimony with them. They must have wondered at such a claim we made of the Lord's blinding power, so he proved it to them, or at least to the pastor's wife Valera and her son Andy who was 11 years old. We had decided to go on a walk and Andy came out looking for us just after we left their house. We saw him and waved at him as he walked by us, but he didn't see us. Then we turned the corner and had only gone a short way, and this time along came Andy and his mother in a car, again like they were looking for us. So we tried to flag them down, we were right before their eyes in a quiet residential street, but they looked at us blindly and headed on, even after pausing right where we were. In the evening when we came back after our walk, the mother asked where we disappeared to <u>so fast</u>! And we told her how we waved at her and her son Andy. We even yelled at them but they didn't seem to hear us. Then they knew <u>for sure</u> that the Lord Jesus <u>could</u> blind people to us because we described exactly when they came by and how they looked, and how her son tried to catch us first, and then came in the car with her. They were astounded! That happened in the bright morning hours. So this pastoral family now knew for sure of the blinding power of God as we did. Praise the Lord! So that is a synopsis of just the tip of the iceberg of a few instances of God's blinding power.

Come to think of it, I want to mention one other profound example for all those "doubting Thomas's" out there. My husband's first name was Thomas so he always said he had to overcome a lot of "doubt" himself. Anyway, this man we met under the bridge in Bakersfield, CA, when we were camping out, was very sick from detoxing from alcohol. He was scared and a brother in the Lord. We sat with him three days and nurtured him and prayed for him as he wanted our company. Each day we would walk with him to McDonalds and we would pass some drunken transients by the railroad tracks. On the third day he wanted to leave and go to a detox center in Seattle, WA, and we agreed to travel with him. So when we passed these ruffian men again they yelled out to him and mumbled under their breath menacingly, that he hadn't told them there was a "woman" with him. Our friend said, "Well I passed by you two days in a row with this couple!" They were shocked. They said, "we saw you, but we never saw that couple." Our friend, the Angel of the Lord, had blinded them once again because they were dangerous men. They saw us on the day we were leaving. So God proved to us and our friend Joe how He protected us mightily in His umbrella of safety.

Chapter 27

ALL OF GOD'S CREATURES SHALL PRAISE HIM! – REVELATIONS 5:13, JOB 12:6-9

A few years before John's health completely failed him, he was starting to really slow down. Rest, rest and more rest, was the best formula! As the backpacking and ailments were taking a toll on dear John, with an ileostomy since he was 24 years old, who was now about 60 years old – (though he looked 43.) Anyway, we were hiding in a lovely little woods by the railroad tracks, behind some condominiums, and the way we first found this spot was by the grace of God. We were in Goleta, a town in sunny California, hidden in the bushes by the tracks when we first saw the hole in the fence. You could hardly see it with all the foliage. We got through that hole in the fence, and much like the "secret garden" there was a beautiful area with very old oak trees and huge walnut trees that looked like they had seven trunks running out of them. We later learned it was an abandoned orchard and so great for "gorilla camping," but wouldn't you know, the first time we stepped through this hole a squawk of great magnitude was heard – and we were trying to be discreet. This *was* gorilla camping after all, not bourgeois camping! So we looked to see what it was – and behind the trees was a fence where these condos were located and hanging on a little porch railing in a large cage, was a huge parrot, very tropical, bright yellow and orange and streams of blue green and aqua. He was beautiful. We both instinctively told him, "Shhh" – and after a few more alarming squawks, he finally quieted down until we got to our spot behind the walnut tree, and put up our tent. He let us know, he was the guardian of the land – "plantation" – so we called him "Henry," which means "guardian of the plantation". So we would often return to this abandoned walnut grove as a resting place and amazingly how smart God's little creatures can be, Henry never squawked at us as we entered again, whether in broad daylight or evening – he would quietly wait until we got to our own spot – and as soon as we had our tent up and were hidden in the trees (and just to show us how smart he was), then he'd start his chatter. He'd say, "helloooo" in a low tone of voice, as in conspiracy with us. And John would say hello back in a low voice. Then he'd say it again and I'd say it back… and on it would go with Henry's brief language knowledge until he was satisfied he'd had a little chat with us… I think he was happy to have company, probably his family was out working or busy inside, and he was happy to see us every time. God inspired this clever bird to comfort us in our sorrow at John's troubling ailments – that were building up in his tired body, and we would rest there two to three days at a time for respite, so he could be revived! Even as we rested – Henry would have a daily chat with us. The neighbors were used to his chatter and didn't think much of it I suppose. But we knew Henry was talking to us! And he wasn't satisfied until we greeted him back with our parrot chatter…

Five years later I'm alone with no Henry in sight, in the same spot, and John, is in Heaven since last year, and I am 52 yrs. old. (And I was actually able to abide in this spot alone for four and a half years, not just three days at a time, and leaving my tent up!) The Lord Jesus sends me a family of scrub jays to comfort me–first I meet Leonard, the male scrub jay, and after a while he brings around his wife mate Gracie… At first I called them all Leonard, but he seemed miffed and brought over Gracie at the same time. They posed for me with their flashing blue feathers as if to say, "Do you get it? There are two of us!"

Next I am thinking of drawing Leonard and Gracie so I do. This is my favorite pastime since my husband graduated to the heavenly realm. I drew a picture of Leonard with his purple head. I show him my pictures and he seems okay about it. I asked the Lord Jesus to fax the picture image of it to him so he can really see it up close (I have lots of faith). So the next thing I know, one day, Leonard comes by with Gracie and a <u>third</u> scrub jay, and I ponder who is this, a sister or what – then as if reading my thoughts – Gracie picks up a piece of cheese and holds it in her mouth. The smaller scrub jay races to steal it from her but she briskly moves away. Immediately the smaller jay morphs into his baby jay behavior and does a fluffing with his wings and heavy squawking and I realize she's their baby and the mother is trying to teach her to eat on her own. There is cheese and bread all over but she wants mom to feed her. Then the three of them seem satisfied and the thought comes to me from the Lord – they want a family portrait, so they brought their child – so I do that and draw all three of them. Amazingly, I saw Maggie, the child, many times after that and she always got her own food with no antics to mom, almost as if she <u>did</u> that to show me that one day, who she was. So that's the story of three little scrub jays and the darling parrot named Henry, who comforted me and John in our sorrow and myself alone later on – the scrub jay that is – Henry was long gone.

And I even wrote a poem about all the other creatures that comforted me and possibly protected me when I was in danger.

The Little Folk
Beneath the canopy of walnut trees, guerilla camping in my little tent...
Feeling the late night breeze through my window vents –
Suddenly, I heard a thud of footsteps move like a person, thud thud thud –
But I listened carefully, my heart racing –
A women alone in a wild place by the railroad tracks –
My husband off to glory a year ago or so –
My heart was in my mouth, and I heard the pregnant pauses, the gentle shifts, but then the thuds – <u>Who was it anyway!</u>
It was the little folk.
"Bernard" as I came to know him, the male skunk –
Letting out his perfume to let me know he was dominant tonight.
Then came his gentle sister, "Tarbell"
She moved with grace and soft-pawed gentile –
No threat was in her step – a little folk with manners!
And then night did fall – some rats did scurry by – but I fed them well and they squeaked their thanks to me in flourishing squeaks of loquacious delight. Especially Bartholomew – head rat I suppose.
Then later in the night I heard a loud thumping –

Thump, Thump, Thump!
I Rose up – my heart racing! Who could it be?
It was Betsy –
Looking gently at me – in the moonlight
A great big possum with large, meek eyes
There she sat munching happily on the leftover fare from
The birds, the skunks the possums and rats, the little folks
Another time, I woke up alone and I couldn't sleep – and I heard a troop
moving through the brush – in pompous flair –
It was early morning and I looked to see
Five baby raccoons and the mother in tow
What a sight, the trendy cloaks of dapper stripes –
The color of autumn, the sweet catlike faces
But wild, untamed, looking right at me
As they paraded by my tent, as if to say –
If you hear us moving through the brush it's only us –
We have to hunt and eat, you see
And Jesus told us you'd like to see us –
The little folk of the woods.
And the little folk of the woods are so illusive, unless <u>they</u> want <u>you</u>
to see them.
So now I sit in my little tent
My ears are fine-tuned to animal events,
I know their steps, their wild moves
Their gentle surreptitious ways of surviving, in the moonlight night
And how they give me comfort in the night –
The quiet munching of Betsy –
The male skunk's familiar smell – don't mess with me –
Even the rat's joyous glee, as they do rat-crobats on a low branch, for a
piece of cheese
Thanking me with squeaks
And my aerial friends in the morning, the bird alarms –
The scrub jays' brilliant blue, coming in to wake me
Squawking merrily to say hi to me, grabbing pieces of bread and dropping them clownishly over and over, to amuse me until I laughed –
No I'm not alone in my little tent,
With my fine feathered friends coming for daylight treats!

A group of tiny little birds with yellow bellies always come in a troupe
To eat the bugs off the large walnut tree leaves twice their size
And the ornately striped woodpecker tapping on my tree
The magnificent walnut tree
Delighting me, the little folk, what a comfort to me
And even the speckled gray birds with peachy color that compete with
the blue jays
All these comfort me as God's glory draws them near, how dear, and
let's them be.

THE LITTLE FOLK, PART 2–THE COMFORT OF GOD

Three months have passed since my first night alone outdoors, when I was introduced to the creatures of the night and day. I rarely see my raccoon friends or possums, elusive as they are – as if to show me it was truly an introduction to let me know everything was okay... but then, one night I'm returning to my little camp-spot, walking down the railroad tracks as the darkness falls. I seldom see a soul, but suddenly from about a block away, up the tracks, as I crossed towards my spot, I see two humans coming up on me – I slip surreptitiously into my spot, through a fence hole – and disappear, feeling my heart beat. Did they see me? Will they follow? I quickly put my tent up and sit and wait – alert to see if they pass on by – perhaps they slipped under the little bridge and went the other way. My eyes become sleepy as I sit and wait – pitch black now – I pray – then suddenly, an explosion of sound – I look over through my tiny window and see movement behind the fence near the railroad tracks. I hear frenetic movement – I grab my heart as I see what looks like dim lights flickering in the night – will they come over the fence? What shall I do? – I pray – Suddenly, there was a big crashing sound and my heart thumping hard – I unzip my door – ready to reveal myself to whomever – then I see an explosion of furry creatures, some running up a tree branch like a possum or a fox, and I see his furry face in the sliver of moonlight – silvery fur like a possum or fox and some raccoons. Others miraculously go up to another tree by me where the bottom of an old broken tree house sits, and lay down. Fuming, I think, they never did that before! Then I smile and chuckle merrily. It's a sign to me! They're on sentry duty for those humans out there tonight. All that noise would scare anybody away. Me and John always said in our many "nature" experiences, "The Lord Jesus will have His Angels to protect us in our "unusual" Calling and he'll even stir up the animal and bird friends, if need be." Well, there it is a <u>graphic illustration</u>! And I am comforted in the night once again by the little folk. My little buddies watching over me again as their ruckus scared the humans away, and I'm alone with my little fold again. Glory be!

My little bird friends are amazing too – my first rainstorm alone I was freaked out, desperately trying to build a gutter around the tent – all by my lonesome self – no dear husband to help me out and encourage me with his lion heart – I sigh – hadn't seen my bird friends either as the weather was changing – my scrub jays who always greeted me in the morning were elsewhere – I missed them.

Suddenly, as the rain takes a break at 5:45pm – in swoops a scrub jay friend – finds a dry piece of bread – and pauses until his spouse comes – and Leonard and Gracie, greet me with their lovely blue feathers shining in the breeze – right on cue! And off they go, and I am comforted for the <u>first</u> rainy night – the obedient birds, sent by God, to comfort me for a long rainy night!!! And I must make honorable mention of my little humming bird friend, Isabel. The humming bird, when it came in real close, always meant to me and John (as God showed us), after he got sick and was less confident, that we were in the "right place at the right time." Well when I was nervous in the service and wanted to leave my camp, but God was telling me to stay and rest for the day – along would come Isabel the hummingbird, and she was good friends with Gracie the scrub jay – they would hover together by my tent. I would be immediately calmed down and realize I was supposed to stay for the day. It was amazing how "in tune" the little creatures of God are!

Chapter 28

Divine Intervention

Psalm 91:9-12–If you make the most high your dwelling – even the Lord who is my refuge – then no harm will befall you, <u>no disaster will come near your tent.</u> For He will command His Angels concerning you – to guard you in all your ways; they will lift you up in their hands, so you will not strike your foot against a stone.

As I sit in my tent alone, a widow of one year and three months, camping out "gorilla style" by the railroad tracks, rain pouring down. And having watched some guy with a backpack walk right by my spot this morning – but he didn't stop – <u>I am grateful how this scripture speaks that no harm or disaster will come near your "tent"!</u> And the Lord is our refuge! My husband and I learned this in our travels. Some mansions could be more frightening to stay in than our little tent, out in the boonies, because our Lord is our refuge – the surroundings do not matter but what is and who is inside of you – the four walls of a house are an illusion of safety – but safety comes from the Lord Jesus Christ. We could testify to that over and over again.

But as I read this scripture, what really comes to my mind is a time when I was riding the freight trains with my husband, and I was always a little nervous when I came into a town that I had to "jump off on the run" – as I never saw myself as especially graceful, like a ballerina, or athletic – as I was sickly as a child – and I couldn't pass the test for ballet at seven; a cartwheel!

Salt Lake City was such a town as this, as we knew the yards was what the tramps called "hot", meaning "the Bull" may pull you off the train or arrest you. So what we did was jump off the train a mile or two before the main yards when the train is, hopefully, creeping along – then you're home free – and out of there (the brakemen, switchmen and engineers were usually glad to slow down and let the human cargo off, as they got a kick out of outfoxing the bull too). So the train got close to the yards and we got ready – I was nervous and praying – John always let me jump first to make sure I didn't get left behind, and if he could help me. This time I got down on a ladder on a grain car – but it was going 15 to 20 miles an hour, which is slow enough, but not easy – so I took a leap but not a good one – and suddenly I felt myself rolling on those rough rocks, right <u>towards</u> the tracks and train wheels – But amazingly an invisible hand or force seemed to push me back so I rolled <u>away</u> from the tracks. My husband John was looking awestruck as he saw how I nearly went off to glory, or lost my legs, right before his eyes – but Somebody – an angel of the Lord intervened and pushed me back – John dear even saw a flash of purest light as I rolled <u>away</u> from the tracks to safety, coming between me and the freight train.

They, the angels of the Lord, kept me from dashing my foot against a stone – a whole freight train!

Chapter 29

BIG FOOT! – EPHESIANS 6 "WE FIGHT NOT AGAINST FLESH AND BLOOD..."

I was reading about a conference on Big Foot in Willow Creek and it brought back an interesting memory in our travels – The time me and John were hitch-hiking up to Patrick's Point, and paused in Eureka on the way, at a McDonalds, where we could rest over a cup of large coffee we shared and get refills. As we rested there, we talked in low voices about some of our revelations and discernments in the Lord Jesus, as we were not into preaching (loudly) indirectly to people – knowing the word of God was a precious pearl – and people will get thirsty around sold-out Christians if they're ready. My husband learned this wisdom from the Holy Spirit. A little while later we vaguely noticed a man observing us closely but we ignored him as we were lost in our talking. Afterwards, we go and hitch-hike and a young man with long hair picks us up, who was going to Patrick's Point! He tells us how he was staying in a huge Quonset hut temporarily with a kind Christian man – and he shared that he knew this man wouldn't mind putting us up for the night, as we were Christians, too. So we go there and he introduces us to this man in the two story Quonset hut right on the ocean by Patrick's Point. Lo and behold, it is the man we saw in McDonalds observing us. "Hey" he says, "I saw you in McDonalds and I noticed your faces were really shining. I knew you were Christians!" So we fellowshipped with this man and eventually met his wife and her sister and their mother. He was a marine biologist professor from Humboldt University and he shared his Quonset hut with college students. The upstairs being like a dorm with bunk beds and the downstairs was a living room and kitchen that were very large. It was empty right then, at its summer break, and the students had left. A new couple was coming in a month to be the older dorm couple over the students. But the professor had to go to Alaska to do some research for his marine biology. He was concerned about leaving the place empty for that month, as some students left on bad terms for breaking rules in the house. So he asked us to care take the place while he was in Alaska, as we really hit it off good with him. His wife's sister and mother remained with us for a little while longer, after he left with his wife for Alaska. Then they left on their trip, too, and we were left alone. They left us with a little food and a little cash and a request to pull out the unruly blackberry bushes in the backyard. It is a beautiful view on a cliff with ocean below, and huge rocks and cormorants and pelicans and other birds and seals dwelling in the ocean to look at while we were doing our work in the yard. We were also left with a great Labrador dog to help us, that the professor had to leave while he was away – and a couple of feral cats that were abandoned – their names were Oso and Raven. Anyway, we were eventually left to ourselves to tend things, and every night the fog rolls in, and we head back into the Quonset hut, after hacking away at these blackberry thorny bushes with ducks and geese running around and a Labrador dog chasing them, by the sea view cliff backyard.

One evening we were outside working and we sensed a strange, eerie presence – my husband and I have the gift of discerning of spirits, I Corinthians 12:10, and we both started seeing wicked spirits manifest. As I recall, I saw some dark spirit and he sees similar manifestations – We feel chills as we note this dark presence which is very large – so we go inside and pray. We go to sleep that night – and my husband suddenly wakes up and sits up in bed and tells me an amazing vision he has. There standing at the foot of the bed he sees a hairy presence 9 feet tall and it says "I am Big Foot". John rebukes it in the name of Jesus. He is wide awake when he sees this and I hear him rebuke it, and it disappears finally, John says.

Well, the next morning he calls up our friend, the professor, in Alaska and tells him the strange happening. This man being Christian, laughs knowingly and tells John over the phone how some neighbors worship Big Foot and got pretty creepy about it – claiming to see it – calling it up, etc. – Crazy! Then we knew that John saw some real entity at any rate. Thanks to the shenanigans of the neighbors who were into such strange witchcraft practices. And we prayed every night after that, more fervently and with relish, knowing Ephesians 6, "We fight not against flesh and blood but wicked spirits in high places."

At night it was pitch black as there were no houses across the street, and it kept us quite prayerful! Which brings to mind another encounter in Santa Cruz, CA, with a young wizard. This gets us into another "occult classic" of another whole topic in the supernatural realm!

Chapter 30

MORE OCCULT ENCOUNTERS WITH WICKED SPIRITS IN HIGH PLACES

Well it's almost Halloween so I may as well tell you some supernatural happenings we had with real witches or occult people – and these people weren't playing around. The Lord Jesus protected us from such encounters like we were in a protected bubble for the first 15 years or so of our walk on the road. A missionary couple who had been to Africa even saw this protective bubble on us in a vision. We had had a few unusual incidences, but nothing really heavy. Then we must have graduated to higher ground, and suddenly we met the real thing.

Our first encounter of a strange kind was in Santa Cruz County, a place diverse with unusual religions. We were at a little mall in Capitola, a town right near Santa Cruz – having a coffee in Carl's Jr. It was there we had our first encounter! John was merrily chatting with me and I with him, about the Lord Jesus, as usual. And then we felt we had stayed there long enough with our one coffee. We headed to the restroom together, packs and all, because we were planning to leave. Lo and behold, we ran into a young man of strange attire, with black hair and fair skin, and as we passed by in the hallway as we were leaving, he glared at us with blatant hostility. John said, "God bless you!" to him and so did I. And next thing we know we're in a battle! He glared at us menacingly and said, "Lucifer loves you." We then noticed that he was wearing priestly black attire to the neck replete with a white collar and chain around his neck with the head of the "wolf." We knew this guy was trouble. John then rebuked him "in the name of Jesus" and so did I. We said, "I rebuke you in the name of Jesus." He actually followed us out of Carl's Jr., as we were leaving, prating and loudly telling us, "you don't know <u>who</u> you are messing with!" And John told him he didn't know who he was messing with either. He kept saying "Lucifer loves you" in a sinister way – and John tells him Galatians 1:8-9, that he's "accursed for preaching another gospel." We head on feeling rather small and insignificant – wondering if we made a dent in that guy's cocky demeanor – with the name of Jesus. John even says to me he felt weak after that attack.

You see, in some power encounters we experienced we knew we hit the mark and even felt God's power. And in other power encounters, like this one, we felt the weakness of God and we were not sure. Well, that night we found out how engaged we were, as we were kept awake in a night vigil, with demonic attacks all night long. Jesus told us this young guy was a little wizard from a generational witch family, and that's why he made it to a wizard so young. A wizard is a head over three covens, from what I've read. He was contacting these covens to attack us in the night to break our faith. And that's why he said "you don't know <u>who</u> you're messing with." It was the spirit of anti-Christ, plain and simple satanic attack. All night long we'd actually see people in visions astro-projecting and trying to terrorize us. We rebuked them all in the name of Jesus, these manifestations of the occult. John, at the same time I was seeing these things, was also seeing similar visions as well – people using demons to astro-project their soul power at you. And we rebuked them until about 3am. We both noticed the game suddenly stopped – silence – and we went into a deep sleep – feeling we had prayed through. Well we started to walk back from Capitola to Santa Cruz. We spent the night under the bridge and rested, exhausted after that attack, and then headed on to Santa Cruz, CA.

Two days later we were at the facility that has MTD busses. We were thinking of taking a bus somewhere towards San Jose, as our elderly friend Jerome had blessed us with $10. So we were sitting on a bench outdoors, resting and checking out the buses, and who do we see but the little guy with his black jacket – same attire, only he has lost his cockiness. He takes one look at us and runs towards his bus, his black jacket tail flapping behind him. Wow, what a difference from two days ago. From a young upstart to a defeated foe – Jesus had the victory! Thank you Jesus. Ephesians 6:11-12 "Put on the whole armor of God, that ye may be able to stand against the wiles of the devil. For we fight not against flesh and blood, but against principalities and powers, against the rulers of darkness of this world, against spiritual wickedness in high places." Hallelujah!

Chapter 31

Testimony of a Drunken Man Set Free

While we're on the subject of Santa Cruz, let me tell you an interesting testimony about a young man we met on a bus going from Santa Cruz to Watsonville – maybe the very bus we took that night after seeing the young guy wizard off. Anyway, I say maybe because we visited Santa Cruz many times in our travels, and remember, we traveled about 24 years or so for the Lord Jesus Christ.

So one day we were on the Santa Cruz bus that takes you the 18 mile journey to Watsonville, which we often had walked as well. While on the bus, a young Native American guy came up to John and me sitting in the back seat quietly with our packs. First, he wanted to shake our hands, but he was falling over drunk, and John refused saying, "No, you're drunk!" So the young guy got mad and threatened to beat us up. John dear, not a natural pacifist, was over-tired and got hot for a moment and wanted to take him on, as he had been walking in the hot sun all day – but the Lord Jesus checked him as he started to feel pugilistic, and I said, "spiritual weapons, John" and so instead John said, "I rebuke you in the name of Jesus." We rebuked Satan in him a few times in the name of Jesus, and he got mad and went up to the bus driver to complain because the bus driver looked like a similar culture to him so he thought he would sympathize. Well it so happens, the bus driver was a Christian, and he told him he was wrong and drunk and ought to apologize. Well we arrived in Watsonville while the young guy was up there talking away, and were we ever relieved to get off the bus. The young Native American got off too. We walked to the grass of the park nearby to rest, and surprisingly the young man followed us so we stopped to hear what he had to say. His face was changed and the drunken arrogance had left. He humbly apologized holding out his hand – saying his real Native American name, which we could tell was precious to him – and asked us to pray for him. We took his hand and prayed for him right there – and later we did more intercessory prayer, for him – And we realized another miracle, that when John and I rebuked him in the name of Jesus, he was set free of the drunken spirit for he was entirely sober then... You see, that's why John wouldn't shake his hand when he was so drunk, because we are intercessors – and you have to pray for them whether you want to or not. Plus, when a person is that drunk the friendliness is false, but in the end it was an authentic friendship. Praise God!

Chapter 32

Language Barrier

While I'm sharing this testimony about the young Native American, I can't help but be reminded of another interesting testimony in our travels. One day, John and I were heading to some freight yards somewhere in Texas, I believe. John was sharing a brand new testimony with me from his past when he traveled 7 years on his own, hitch-hiking across the country back and forth. Just then my ears perked up – we had been together about 8 years and I had never heard this one!

John started telling me about one time when he was witnessing with another brother in Christ to some people that were interested – and there were some Native Americans standing nearby in a group. Although he wasn't even talking to them, they started cussing him out in their native tribal tongue. At first, John told me, he didn't know what to do. But the Holy Ghost came upon him and enabled him to speak in his spiritual language – in "tongues" or glossolia, as the theologians say. He spoke out loud to them and immediately they all calmed down and became peaceful. "Wow," I said to John, "what a good idea. You never told me that!" I thought to myself, when another person verbally attacks you in their own language and you don't understand it, why <u>not</u> speak in your spiritual language. As soon as John told me this, the Holy Spirit spoke to me and said – "John's telling you this because you're going to be needing this revelation soon!"

Sure enough, we did! As we headed down to the docks of the warehouses where the freight trains go by – and we sat on the docks of a warehouse in the early evening, waiting for a train to catch –Along came one – stopping dead – going just the way we intended to go. But alarmingly, off the train came a whole bunch of illegal aliens from Mexico, who must have traveled together, about 6 guys, and walked right over to us and surrounded us, closing in, speaking in violent guttural Spanish language as they grew closer and closer, surrounding us – And some sat by us on the dock, way too close (on the road this is never done, everybody keeps their distance unless they want to hurt you), as the others were moving in. Suddenly, John and I looked at each other and knew just what to do as they jabbered in an unknown tongue to us – we started to speak in our heavenly language back to them – the both of us! Well, it was amazing – the shekinah glory must have come down because within minutes they were laughing as if we had just given them a bottle of wine – we did – "new wine"! I mean this was joyous, friendly laughter, not mocking. And they came up to us with their hands out and started talking – lo and behold, in <u>English</u> – asking us where we were going, shaking our hands as if we were old buddies. It was great! "Well, we're going to catch that train that <u>you</u> just got off," we said. So we got on the nearest grain car – and they all waved at us, smiling and happy, and we waved back like we were all best friends – and we were – Jesus was there and he brought instantaneous love and oneness – You notice, I said oneness and not unity, because unity like the military is usually forced or contrived like a club – but oneness is "supernatural"! Remember in Acts 2:4-11, when they spoke in tongues, everyone heard it in their <u>own language</u>, and there were quite a few cultures there that day! – So I often wondered what these men heard when <u>we</u> spoke in that unknown language – the Lord Jesus must have translated it for their ears and set them free, to higher ground – much like in Acts where everyone heard the tongues in their own language – a miracle!

Chapter 33

Hostility Diffused by the Holy Spirit

Another time in Texas, we ran into these Texas ranchers – via a Pentecostal church a former sheriff had invited us to. The pastor especially wanted us to meet them because they were fairly new converts and rough around the edges. This particular pastor recognized our Calling in Christ Jesus. Although these two men had been in the church for a long time, they had learned to be in the Spirit recently through this new church. So they had lots of machismo and legalism to overcome. They needed some help on their ranch so we did some work with them – and we came in the evening for fellowship at their dinner table. These two brothers were big guys like Hoss on "Bonanza"–quite the traditional macho men you might expect in Texas. Well we watched them with their wives and they boasted about their little women as they served the meal obediently. They also talked about their friend who was going to jail for killing his wife's lover. Their friend was born-again, but in the heat of passion he did this deed of violence when he caught them together. So the big Texan guys asked us to pray for their friend who was there visiting before he headed to jail. First John, my husband, prayed. Then I felt led to pray too, but I felt such macho misogyny and legalism in the air (like women be silent), but yet I knew I was inspired – so I prayed in an unknown tongue first to break this barrier and build up my spirit and have courage to pray. Well the tongue came out amazingly beautiful like an oriental tongue I had seldom heard before. I finished and then felt released to speak a prophesy I had for this man, and it rolled right out of me and comforted the brother in Christ exceedingly, who was facing jail and prison soon. Later on, the big Texan brothers laughed and said, "When she prayed in tongues I felt like a few devils were jumping out of me all over the place." And

John and I laughed because we knew that when I spoke in my heavenly language, the Holy Spirit was battling the machismo dominant spirits right out of the way, to clear the way, to give that refreshing word like refreshing waters to comfort that dear brother. As Ephesians 6:12 says, we fight against the unknown.

Nazi-Guy Encounter

Another incident where the power of the Lord Jesus diffused hostility happened in LA County. We were walking through a busy city with our backpacks at night, and the street was bustling. A white guy with a Nazi zig-zag haircut took one look at our despicable backpacks, and started mouthing off hateful words of violence like a real predator – as we didn't fit in with his agenda of what he thought was "normal". First we God blessed him, but he continued to mouth off! This time, we rebuked <u>him</u> in the name of Jesus – I recall John said, "I rebuke you in Jesus name," and I rebuked him as well. He suddenly shut up and started laughing and said, "Hey, hey I know what you guys are doing" and he chatted with us amicably, for a bit, and with pure joy, shook our hands and was on his way! It was profound – like Jesus had lifted the demon of hatred right off of him – and reminded him, possibly, of his own Christian roots – and melted his little ol' pea-picking heart, as Tennessee Ernie Ford used to say – John and I were very happy and headed down the road singing a song about Jesus our King – He is Master of everything! Praise the Lord!

Chapter 34

A String of Pearls

Being anxious can't add one cubit(18 in.) to your height... but –

Luke 12:25

Not to refute the scriptures – it's true – being "anxious" <u>can't even</u> add one inch to your height – <u>but</u> I was sickly as a child with asthma and the Lord Jesus healed that – but I always remember the doctor's saying when I was 7 years old that the medication I took for asthma must have stunted my growth, with a chuckle yet. Well, ha ha, I was the shortest in my class at the time. And the doctor even added, "I think you need growing pills, ha ha." So I told my husband at about 26 years old that I thought I should be taller – after all John was 5'11", and after, when he had his ileostomy operation at 24 years old he had grown in 3 years from 5'8" to 5'11". So John, a man of faith, prayed that I'd grow. I was 5'1 ¾" and I suggested that he pray for 5'5". So he prayed for me and the next time I measured myself I <u>was</u> a whole inch taller! So how about that! <u>If</u> you <u>pray</u>, you <u>can</u> add an inch to your height!

Now some deliverances of demons or diseases come out only by prayer and fasting – Matthew 17:14-21, Luke 9:39, Mark 9:17-25. I was reading about these three similar accounts about a child tormented by a demon in which Jesus called out a deaf and dumb spirit, and also a lunatic in another account – but at any rate, it struck me how the child being thrown down – foaming, writhing, etc – was a lot like epileptic fits. The disciples failed to deliver this child, a man's son, and so he was brought to Jesus – who later rebukes the disciples in Matthew 17 for unbelief, but added "this kind doesn't go out but by prayer and fasting"

– Then I recalled an event, my husband shared with me as a young apostle prophet in his early travels. He was in Juarez, Mexico – where he had been invited in his wanderings to stay with these Christians involved in a Bible school and orphanage. John was with them awhile and given what amounted to a little closet to stay in with no running water. He didn't care since he was a traveler for Jesus. The elders of this group of Christians were concerned about an epileptic man they had needed to pray for a number of times. He had hoped Jesus would deliver him, so John meanwhile, began to pray and fast – for reasons unknown to him, except that the Holy Spirit had dealt with him to do so. He was on about his fifth day of fasting – when this poor young man had an epileptic fit in the morning hours. Well, the brothers in this place surrounded him, rebuked the devil, and prayed for healing – to no avail. Then along came John and he felt the Lord's prompting to pray for him. So he asked if he could and they agreed. So he walked up to the man having a fit and says, "I rebuke the spirit of epilepsy (as he could see it) in Jesus' name." Well lo and behold, out it came, and the man became peaceful as a baby and was healed according to the men. He did not suffer any more seizures after that – and this showed how prayer and fasting can facilitate your faith <u>for deliverance</u>!

By the way, after the powerful prayer, John a young guy to them in his 30's, was suddenly promoted from a closet room without water to a larger room with running water for the rest of his stay! And that was a happy ending – Praise the Lord Jesus! Like I read in Psalm 75:6-7, we are <u>not</u> to promote ourselves but the Lord promotes us in <u>His</u> <u>time</u>. This is the simplicity of the gospel. We are not to strive for honor – like "selfish ambition" – but you do "press through" for the prize of the High Calling in Christ Jesus, through obedience, which brings "dominion" as in power in prayer and fasting, in speech, in persevering in preaching, etc., <u>and</u> being your "authentic self" in a daily holy walk.

Chapter 35

Heavenly Success

Considering 1 Corinthians 13:5, that love has no ambition,-not self-seeking/ NIV- that brings to mind the often polarized opposite of "worldly success" which is "Heavenly Success."

We would always pray for "Heavenly Success" when we entered into new situations or battles – knowing full well this might mean appearing to be a failure to the world – but having spiritual victory as a result, like Jesus our Lord dying on the cross, but rising to victory with resurrection power

My husband had an encounter before he met me at a Hawaiian "Rescue mission". He was staying there in his travels helping out in the ministry of the word of God and other humble tasks, when a man walked up on him and started cussing up a storm and taking Jesus' name in vain. John told him, "Go outside if you're going to cuss, as this is the Lord's house." But the man kept it up saying he didn't have to because it wasn't a church. John continued and said, "I'm a temple of the Holy Spirit and this building is for the Lord Jesus' work!" So the man threatened to beat him up and even said, "Let's take it outside!" And John said, "If you want to do anything, you'll have to do it right here!" The man punched him a couple times and hit him hard in the jaw. John did not fight back, as the scriptures teach "turn the other cheek." The man said, "Go ahead and hit me back." John told him, "I won't lift my little finger to touch you – my Heavenly Father will take care of you!" And the guy took off in a huff.

John looked like a failure – one young Christian guy even mocked him saying he was just showing off – though later, he was convicted and had to apologize to John for saying that. Meanwhile, John's jaw was throbbing and a little later he was sitting in a café and a sister in the Lord saw him sipping a coke and brought him a big hero sandwich. He thanked her but then sat and looked at it. His jaw was in such pain that he couldn't open it but he was ravenously hungry. He cried, "Oh Lord Jesus, I stood up for you and I can't even eat this sandwich." Suddenly he had an uncontrollable urge to yawn. He even tried to stop it because he was afraid of the pain – but he yawned nonetheless, his eyes tearing, and it snapped back in place. His jaw was dislocated before that, but Jesus healed his jaw and he could eat his sandwich.

He later learned that the young man who had challenged him, and hit him, had, in a short time of that incident, like a month, lost his wife, his home, and his job and everything went downhill for him. God was knocking on his door for his mockery and he learned "touch not my anointed and do my prophets no harm" Ps.105:15, – he was paying for mocking God! And His servant, John.

Powerful Discernments

Matthew 16:19 and 18:18, "And whatsoever you bind on earth shall be bound in Heaven."

One of the gifts of the Holy Spirit, 1 Corinthians 12:8-10, besides the gift of tongues, healing and miracles – is the gift of "discerning of spirits." My husband had it ever since he was 12 and got saved, at a Kathryn Kuhlman evangelistic meeting in Pittsburg, Pennsylvania. With this gift, John could tell if a preacher was lying or being deceiving, backslidden, or under the pure Holy Spirit anointing – if the Holy Spirit so chose to open up his eyes. He would have an open-eyed vision, or discernment, when he'd see, for instance, a black spirit coming out of a liar's mouth – or purest light for God's anointing for truth – or sometimes blue silver light for God's anointing. A goldish light was deception and a black light was outright wickedness. I was prayed for, by John, to receive his gift of discerning of spirits and eventually, I too was blessed with spiritual visions – in a different way than John, as the Holy Spirit had us fitted together as a perfect complement to each other. We each helped the other out in discerning things as a husband and wife team. The Lord Jesus especially blessed me in visions. Often while I was resting I could see a vision of a spirit that worked through someone I had met and I'd bind it up in Jesus' name. One time I had a real graphic illustration – right before my eyes!

I was in Klamath Falls, Oregon, and sitting at a dinner table with various Christians. There was one woman who was older and sickening sweet to me and John, and highly religious in her attire – some sort of nun's garment, though she was <u>not</u> a Catholic. I did not feel at ease with her – so I left the table and after dinner sat by a wood burning fire as the door was opened up. Us hobos loved our fires – the hobos or "tramps" call it "old time TV" as they entertain themselves under bridges on cold winter nights having some pleasant home made coffee made with grounds. So back to my fiery mediation – suddenly I had an open-eyed vision, right in front of my eyes I saw a perfect view of a "skunk" – there was even bluish sky behind it. I thought – isn't he cute – what does that mean, Lord? The Lord Jesus spoke to me clearly – "This is about the woman you are ill at ease with – she acts cute and fluffy to you and John but she will stink you up." Wow, I thought, what'll I do – and I was told by the Lord Jesus to bind up the "skunk" spirit in her – and I did so in Jesus name.

I came to understand that the animal kingdom was sometimes used by the Lord God as a metaphor to describe the attributes of evils spirits working through people. Although, sometimes animals could represent good things too! So this was God's secret code to us in spiritual warfare.

Sure enough this elderly woman raised up a stink about us behind our back – but because the spirit of gossip, represented by a skunk, was bound up, my husband and I had power over it, as well as other people. When you bind up an evil spirit on somebody, it becomes obvious and stupid. People told on her and she gossiped to the wrong ones – noble people who had integrity this time – and because they had heard our testimony, and it had bore witness to them, they rebuked her. So that's how it works. Even if it's a church pastor, deacon, elder, person on the street or anybody, if God revealed to us that it was a "snake", for instance, we knew we had to bind it up immediately so that it wouldn't have power over us to hurt us. And then it became obvious instead of subtle, and we were able to put it in its place – even the person who <u>had</u> the evil spirit, had to see it more clearly once it was bound up in Jesus' name. Remember how Jesus called the Pharisees "snakes"; well he was disarming them by exposing the wicked evil spirit in them to the light. So that's two ways to deal with evil spirits in the predatory nature in men – 1. Bind it up in prayer in Jesus' name, or 2. Call them on it. We could have said for example, "You lied to everyone about us, you skunk!" But we didn't have to, as others rebuked her for us. Other times we did though. As Mt.18:18 says, "Whatsoever you bind in earth shall be bound in heaven." And we are also told to expose the unfruitful works of darkness. So there you have it, Ephes. 5:11-13, NIV.

Chapter 36

Binding the Strong man

Now the Lord Jesus took us a little deeper into the spiritual battle later on. Much later in life, John received a gift of the Holy Ghost from a saintly woman in England – that was an increase of his gift of discerning of spirits, he already had, and later he prayed I would receive this one too. Jesus said you must bind up the strong man in order to take the house. So we wondered how this new discerning of spirits gift would manifest. John had gotten into plenty of hot water, as you can imagine. His initial gift was like the urim and thummin, which means light and power – that revealed the truth or a lie.

This new gift manifested at an unusual little church group in Southern California that we attended. We were sitting at a home prayer meeting and a heavy-set woman seemed to be the queen of the prayer meeting. She had been exalted very quickly, mainly because of her religious heritage. But as we observed all the fanfare – my husband and I failed to get the witness of the Holy Spirit on her. She was boisterous and pushy and not a restful soul to be around. My husband was observing her while she tried to push people down in prayer and saw her actually turn into a huge spider from head to foot. We had visions of spiders before, representing coldness or witchcraft, but this was different, because the spirit actually took over her entire being and she turned into a spider. Next, John was observing quietly in the fellowship, as she was acting high and holy, she turned also into a cockroach from head to toe – in an open-eyed vision. Wow, we thought, that means she's low down and dirty. So together we bound up these wicked spirits in her, quietly in the name of Jesus, so they would become obvious to all. Well she started praying for people, laying hands on them, and they'd fall down under some sort of power, but we realized this was a counterfeit. Her evils spirits were creating this phenomenon and not the Holy Spirit. Although we had seen and experienced the authentic "slaying in the spirit" as it's called, John would see a beautiful anointing when it was authentic – sometimes like a Turkish sword 150 feet long of blue silver light like he saw at Katherine Kuhlman meetings as a young man, and she would say, "I see the glory of the Lord all over this place," and bunches of people would fall down under the slaying power of the Holy Spirit, with nobody touching them. Anyway, this woman was mad that <u>we</u> didn't fall down under <u>her</u> power, when we all held hands for prayer from her. The meeting broke up and she was already whispering against us to the pastor and his wife, and we hadn't said a word against her.

John was stunned with what he saw that time, but later we did share what we saw with the pastor and his wife, whose home we stayed in. We were allowed to testify in this church, as well, and share with the congregation and even sang a few songs and were well received. Well, this prayer leader woman became very jealous and this is how the "cockroach" manifested. In a week, suddenly the "sound system" was missing – quite a large piece of equipment. Immediately, this high and mighty woman started to accuse us, behind our backs, to several people including the pastor – saying those homeless bums must have took it. (Interestingly, she and others had keys to the church, we didn't!) These people were kind enough to tell us the gossip she had said, and they were astounded at her stupidity, as we only had backpacks and no car, so how could we steal such a huge piece of equipment. But that's because the cockroach, "low down and dirty spirit," was bound up, as well as the "cold-hearted spider"; this makes it stupid in its wisdom. She was rebuked by several people for her foolish talk and once more the Holy Ghost exonerated us by having us ahead of the game, through divine intercession. Praise the Lord Jesus! And as John and I later came to understand, when an evil spirit, such as we saw on her, manifests over the entire being and <u>not</u> just off to the side, that means the demon is entirely in them and they are not even saved, though they may claim to be. As Jesus says, "Except you bind up the strong man, how can you take the house." So hopefully, someday she truly got saved, as the Lord

Jesus broke her down from these demonic strongholds in her life – now exposed and bound up.

So, there you have several examples of Heavenly Success through prayer. Meekness isn't weakness. Matthew 12:28-29, "But if I cast out devils by the Spirit of God, then the Kingdom of God is come unto you. Or else, how can one enter into a strong man's house, and spoil his goods, except he first <u>bind the strong man</u>? And then he will spoil his house."

Chapter 37

BOXCAR EPISODES

Well we had some very interesting experiences in homes with the Lord Jesus Christ, but we always returned to the boxcars. And that's where we spent most of our time traveling, living, ministering and praying.

I remember a time the Lord Jesus delivered us from a terrible storm, via a boxcar, and were we ever grateful! We had walked over the bridge from Vancouver, Washington, to the Portland, Oregon side. It was raining, and as there was a small yard nearby, we got into the nearest boxcar. We didn't care if it went anywhere at that point – just so we stayed dry, as it was raining profusely. Well we got our tarp and rubber mats laid out and our sleeping bags, and we were cuddling real close, so happy to be warm. Suddenly the old car knockers came along – which means you're not going to stay put for the night. We were exhausted and didn't care and felt at peace. We found ourselves moving in a fairly small train out of the yards. Oh great, we thought, we're going somewhere! We went into a deep sleep at the calming sound of the rain and rumble of the freight train. We heard some serious winds blowing but we felt safe and sound. We woke up at 3am or so, and noticed we were in a very dark place. It looked like a warehouse. We fell back asleep, too exhausted to care. We woke again at about 5am and a few dim lights were on so we could see we were in a warehouse and a couple of workers wandering around in the distance in a different area. Me and John looked at each other in a moment of shock. Our boxcar had been dropped off in a warehouse, while we slept! "Let's try to get out of here," John said. So we gathered our stuff, 1 -2 -3 and we high-tailed it out of there in the dimly lit warehouse, praying that God would <u>blind</u> the workers to us, and praying for an <u>open</u> door. We found an unlocked side door and were afraid the fenced yard might be locked since it was early, but praise God there was an exit, and we slipped out of there as quietly as a couple of Bengal tigers escaping a snare. We went out into the streets of Portland – now in the main city. We probably had gone about a 5 to 7 mile ride, but we saw how the Lord Jesus had protected us in that warehouse and boxcar. The wind was still whipping up though the rains had slowed way down. We had escaped a fierce storm and trees were broken all over as we walked the streets. We saw a terrible mess of debris that had flown all over the place. We got to the nearest McDonalds to share a large cup of coffee, shivering with pure joy as we got many refills, and hearing about the terrible storm that had hit, and how we were protected in the great hands of the Living God – who moved us about like his chess pieces in the storm. The storm subdued eventually and we caught out of the Portland yards a little further down, to avoid the "Bulls", in a nearby town, and that took us all the way back to Klamath Falls, Oregon – a nice long ride.

∽

Another interesting boxcar experience we had, in the same yards by Portland, gave us another surprise. Again, a small train that we had got on, didn't take us very far, but dropped us off in a little island area – an electrical island. We were sleeping again, as we woke up and they dropped us off. Hearing the familiar suction sounds of the air being let out when the train stops, we noticed we were stranded. Getting out, at <u>night</u> time, groggy with sleep, we gathered our stuff to see where we landed in the middle of the night. It seemed to be an electrical plant, island. At first we thought of going back to a piece of the train that would possibly be heading out, but John dear said to me, "Maybe we can sleep here." It had very dense growth and bushes and woodsy areas. So we headed down the road on a little adventure, looking for that "perfect" spot the Holy Ghost would give us peace at. John would actually sometimes see a beautiful anointing of light manifest that was for the right place. But instead, we both felt edgy and finally just stopped in a little area of trees, just to pause and rest. It was very dark, not much around us except woods and the plant was far off. Suddenly we heard a blood-curdling howl that pierced the night air and made our hair stand up – it was so chilling. It was not quite a wolf's howl but it was sub-human, yet human. Talk about thrills and chills. When it stopped it seemed like an eternity. It sounded like a wild man or a werewolf! Well, we prayed fervently for a little bit, and then with no peace left, John and I decided to get out of there! And so we headed back to a boxcar that had engines on it, and in a few hours we were checking out of there – happy to stay put for a while.

So that's the way of the freight trains, you never know where you are going to land or <u>who</u> you're going to meet. Whoever, or whatever, that was, it was our ticket out of there. Sometimes God gave us staying power and fearlessness to fight powers and principalities that would attack us through people, but if the Lord's peace departed we were gone like the wind. "A wise (prudent) man foreseeth evil and hides himself, but the foolish(simple) pass on and are punished." Proverb 22:3

Another time we caught a freight train ride all the way to Red Oak, Iowa. John was tempted to visit some old friends that he had to rebuke about something very serious, but the Lord Jesus showed him "no!" He told me so, but unbeknownst to me, John had secretly changed his mind – getting in his affections for these people (crucify you affections and lusts [Galatians 5:24] and set your affections on things above [Colossians 3:2]) – and so he turned down the street heading towards where his old friends lived. But suddenly, a car came up on us in this little residential street. These pasty looking white guys who looked quite high on drugs, spoke in drawling voices as they slowed their car down to talk to us. "Say, you want a ride down memory lane," they said. We were already answering "no" as they concluded what was obviously a weird way to ask for a ride. So John and I stopped in our tracks – and what a shock! Suddenly the car stops in this quiet street with no traffic, and this guy comes running out with an axe (my mind flashed to "Friday the 13th, though I never saw that one, thank God!). Meanwhile, John is standing there like a little lamb as the guy runs right towards him, axe poised above his head. I stepped in front of John and pointed at this man, and said, "I rebuke you in the name of Jesus!" (I might have added – I rebuke you "Satan" in the name of Jesus). But anyway, he stopped cold – axe poised just above John's head, frozen – stopped! He slowly dropped his axe – turning heel and headed back, as he said in his slow drawl, looking back at us, "Jesus never did <u>anything</u> for me." – "Well, He <u>did</u> today!" I said, my voice shaking. "Yeah!" laughed John, "He did today, buddy!" And off he went, in his car leaving us alone. John then explained to me how he was heading down the street to see his friend in disobedience. God had warned him they were still angry, because we had rebuked a relative of theirs. John knew it was a metaphor that they would do a "hatchet job" on him.

So, when John was having a low day – the Lord Jesus used me – a mere woman – to defend John with the Lord's weapon and power! When John was caught in "memory lane", which would have been hazardous to our health! Praise the Lord Jesus Christ!!! Thank you Jesus! Needless to say, John was convinced not to go down memory lane and meet someone with an axe to grind!

Chapter 38

SLICE OF OUR LIFE – THE LIFE OF RILEY

Boxcars are great places for resting in – "boxcar therapy." I can remember us catching a freight train out of Las Vegas – putting our mat out with tarp and sleeping bag, in the far corner, and then just resting with my dear husband as the train headed on the long ride to Salt Lake City, Utah, hearing the pleasant sound of the clickety-clack of the railroad tracks, putting us into a deep sleep. And when we had a little stove on us – (often a homemade one made out of a can and chicken wire, using little sticks for fuel. Or other times we had a Coleman one burner stove and would use cheaper gas, i.e., unleaded fuel instead of white gas). We'd heat up some pizza on a tin can that we found in the dumpster, and make a little coffee! Ah, hobo heaven – right when the boxcar was moving. It was so lovely. That was a fairly long ride to Salt Lake City – And we arrived all chipper and rested up and jump off in Salt Lake City, and let the Lord Jesus use us however He wanted to. Often, if we had some spare change, we'd catch a local bus to Ogden, Utah, for a couple of dollars – which is called a *Jack-Mormon town* – because they are less uptight about rules than the capital city town of Salt Lake City. You see, a lot of Jack-Mormon's live there, that is those that like to jump the rules, like no drinking, like jack-rabbits, but still wish to remain Mormon – so they're called Jack-Mormon. Transients can feel the difference. It is definitely more kick-back in Ogden, and we always found great camping spots, and we'd get some great food out of the local Hardy's dumpster.

One winter in our many times in Ogden, Utah, we camped out for about 3 weeks in an abandoned hotel, with a bed mattress on the floor for us. Quite comfortable – and we locked the door. It was easy access every day, and very comforting to the lowly lifestyle of a railroad tramp. We enjoyed every minute of it, as it was freezing cold in the winter time. One time while there, John and I came down with colds, and it was zero degrees in the daytime, and we said let's go to the local Rescue mission. So we did. Well, we had a dinner and it was okay – fairly simple, like beans and rice – and then before that we had church – this mission made you go to church before the meal, because some just came for the meal and they wanted to make sure you got preached to. It was sad they did it that way, but we were already saved so it didn't bother us. So we spent the night in a communal sleeper's room, and they split us up of course – I was with the women and John with the men. We were woken up at the crack of dawn, in the guise of encouraging us to work, and we went out in the freezing cold street, after only a little coffee and a piece of donut. Wow, was it cold! Where to go? We found a local mall – to go to get warmed up in – that happened to leave the inside opened early before the stores were opened. It was such a relief as we were freezing, with snow on the ground and below zero. Well, after a while we were sitting on some little blocked areas for sitting, and a fast food place finally opened up in the mall. So we had enough change to get a coffee and share it, and then we headed down to the library that opened up around 9 or 10am, to warm us up some and rested there, reading magazines and books. Our colds weren't any better, as you can guess, but after that night at the mission, even though we could stay two more nights, we said, "Forget this, let's go back to the place we slept. At least we can sleep until the sun warms us up." So we did, and slept very well, with "body heat" together. As it says in Ecclesiastes 4:11, wisely, "two in the bed make heat!" (LVB) And we woke up feeling much better after that cold morning wandering around, and we slept in until 9am, and headed outdoors, getting to the library by 10am, Praise the Lord! The life of a hobo is all about survival and it isn't always easy! Though it has its moments!

Chapter 39

ANIMAL ENCOUNTERS...
A "BEAR" MESSENGER

One time when we were in the area of Portola, California – where we had attended a little Baptist church, I mentioned before, where John had asked, "Do you let bums worship here who love Jesus?" And as I said, the pastor received us gladly and asked us to testify. Anyway, we were arriving on another visit, and arrived by freight train, as usual. The freights would drop us off right in Portola, no problem. It gets cold up there – we're talking about a pine tree area with a river running by – very pretty, but cold. So we had visited this little Baptist church and felt led to intercede for them because they were going through a crisis – and that was one of our functions in our Calling – intercession. But as we set up camp in this beautiful woodsy area, and nestled in the pines under the cold, starry sky in our little tent – we had some second thoughts about praying. We'd lay in each other's arms all cozy, talking about the day's events, and started to drift into a sweet sleep.

Suddenly, around midnight, we heard a great roar – we both sat upright in this dark forest! A bear! Another roar, that was closer yet. John said in a shaking voice, "The Lord had told me to pray for this church and I was going to forget about it, as I was tired, but I guess we'd better." At that, we hustled out of the tent, and made a big bonfire – and spoke in tongues – quite easily for at least two hours! "Lester", the bear – that's what we called him – never bothered us again, needless to say. He had done his job for the Lord, waking up two lazy prayer warriors. Later that day, the pastor of the church told us he had just gone bear hunting! So we knew we had definitely encountered a "bear"! And that's the story of how a bear was used to keep us on track, and I'm sure that bear will go to Heaven for doing its job! At least we prayed he would. Meanwhile, the crisis of the church was diverted in quite a miraculous way. So we were glad we prayed! Thanks to Lester!

…A Coyote Tiff

That reminds me, another time we were in Indio, California – sleeping out in the warm desert night – a ways out there so as to avoid the more populated transient areas in Indio that were popular, as the last area we checked was very rowdy. The freight trains ran right through it on the way to Yuma, Arizona, coming from Colton, California. Anyway, we were "out" in the desert with no tent, on a warm night. Well suddenly, while we were dozing off, eerie coyote sounds surrounded us. And as we were being surrounded, my mind flashed quickly to encounters I read about wolves doing just that, in *Island of the Blue Dolphins* – so I was mighty nervous! For some reason, all we could think to do was pray in tongues (our spiritual language) out loud at them as they were quite vocal. Amazingly, they stopped their howling, and after a quiet period we heard them scamper off. We always joked – those coyotes understand tongues! And the Lord knew just what to say to a gang of coyotes!

The next day we visited the transients who were living on the edge of town with pretty nice partial shacks and stoves that were homemade. Quite a nice setup – but we were still glad we slept out with the wild coyotes, as my husband always protected me, a female, from the "coyotes" in men – as he knew what was in the hearts of man – being one himself – especially a heavily drinking group! So we usually soloed it sleeping out with each other – preferring the company of wild animals – under the starry sky – who are sometimes more obedient to God than men.

…Divine – Ahem! – And Magpie Intervention

Well, while we're on the subject of creatures, here's a couple for the birds.

I was riding the freight trains with my dear beloved John and ended up in some little town up north – where the magpies are plentiful – like

North Dakota. We were asleep in a little abandoned shack, that the Lord had led us to out in a field one night in the cold night – And as you know, it's hard to get up in the morning without a heater. So we were hugging our down sleeping bags to us, and in zooms a magpie right through the open window (that had no glass), and raised a raucous. Finally, we felt somehow alarmed to get up, gathered our stuff, and headed outside, and within seconds some rowdy people pulled up that may have caused us trouble – and we missed them by a hair – Thanks to our little Birdie messenger.

The second time these flying black and white magpies came in handy we found some boxcars that were empty on the railroad tracks–and grabbed one to sleep for the cold night. We woke up around 6 am – resting in each other's arms blissfully (cold weather is very romantic) and not intending to get up for awhile – and along comes a magpie again. This one flies right into our boxcar – raising a ruckus until we got up – John was even saying, "Get out of here!" – But he wouldn't until we got up! Suddenly, remembering that former magpie experience, we gathered our stuff. No sooner had we done that, we saw heading down the tracks with his little billy club, the railroad Bull – checking out every boxcar for tramps, a real stickler with nothing else better to do – So sensing an uncomfortable encounter, we hopped to the opposite side of the tracks discreetly as his back was turned to us – and hurried off railroad property to head on out to town, just in the nick of time.

Life as a hobo – never a dull moment! And I for one, love magpies! Some farmers hate them because they peck at sheep. When the state of Montana was going to make them the state bird – the farmers protested because they peck on sheep (or lambs). That does sound awful, but to me and John, they were "St. Magpie"! And we prayed they'd go to Heaven, at least those two, who helped us avoid trouble – and a few others did two. Well, crows and ravens are at the top of the encyclopedia list of most intelligent birds, believe it or not. So, I imagine the Angel of the Lord, finds some ready helpers in the little magpie, related to the crow – which's bigger than a blue jay, and quite lovely sitting on the snow – flashing black and white, on a cold winter day, as they take off.

Chapter 40

DIVINE AND ANGELIC HEAVENLY-WINGED INTERVENTION

John and I often noticed when the demons were troubling a soul. As we shared our testimonies of God's intervention and protection – they would suddenly whip out their weapon, as if to say "I'm tough too and I can beat your a** any time." Their weapons were carnal and ours were spiritual. We'd usually be telling the person how we rebuked someone in the name of Jesus, and it stopped that person cold – So one time we shared with this young man, by a bus depot (outdoor facility) about how we rebuked dangerous people in the name of Jesus. Suddenly, the young guy started flipping his feet around, and showing off his karate moves. Then he aimed a kick right at John's face, but stopped his foot sideways, inches before John's face – hoping, of course, that John would wince or grimace in fear and pull back. But John was as peaceful as an angel – and told me later that he saw the foot coming at him in slow motion and could have grabbed it if he wanted to, but also, the Angel of the Lord was there too, and he saw a flash of light, that the Angel of the Lord was blocking his fancy footwork from harming John – or even disturbing him – as this would have been a sign of weakness, after giving our powerful testimonies in the Lord.

John dear, was always a great warrior for Jesus and always knew how to be fearless and calm in battles – and it helped me greatly, to be calm as well… because "perfect love casts out fear" 1 John 4:18, and that is an atmosphere of faith – <u>where the Lord can work</u>!

The next incident that was a graphic illustration of angelic intervention happened at a church in the <u>South</u>, that was Pentecostal – The Bible

Belt – A nice older couple invited us to their home and wanted to hear our testimonies, so John and I were sitting on the couch, sharing how we had rebuked this person and that person, in the name of Jesus, and how sometimes we rebuked Satan in them in the name of Jesus, as well, if the person was really violent...

This young man, their son, was there, who was about 20 years old, and very low in his spirit, as his youthful marriage had failed and he had even been suicidal. He was sullen and rather disturbed that we were even there at all, and started flipping his sumari type sword around. His mother explained that he had known karate and sumari swordsmanship, since he was 15 years old. He got closer to us as we shared our testimonies, whipping this sword around with great skill, but getting pretty scary around us. This time he flipped the sword inches from our faces, and a holy calm was on both of us and neither of us flinched. It was one warrior against another warrior (the Lord) and he showed that young man in an instant that what we shared was real – and our testimonies were not just mere talk. I'm sure his mother would have corrected him if he wasn't so fragile, but she had held her peace when he started to swing his sword around. At that instant our lives were in the Lord's hands – and after that demonstration, the young man ceased his troubling ways, as we had passed our test, and we were given a restful night there, and he was hospitable and friendly to us after that as well.

When John and I took off a year in Sacramento – working and living in an apartment – we had no TV or anything, so for entertainment we'd walk downtown and see a special of three movies for a dollar. They were almost always karate movies – we saw all the champions – Bruce Lee, Chuck Norris – and some of those really old-fashioned movies with older Chinese men with super karate skills. We were often the only "Anglos" in the movie theatre audience. Anyway, the young guy would always try to beat up on the old guy who had this reputation. The older guy would be drinking his little flask of alcohol and his longish white hair would make him look weak. But the older guy was not just quick, he was supernatural. The young guy would be flaying his arms wildly and the older guy wouldn't blink an eye, but would knock the young guy down <u>without</u> lifting a finger! The idea was, he was so fast you couldn't see him move. John and I would always laugh – "That's like Holy Ghost karate," we'd always say – "He moves so fast you can't even see he moved." Praise the Lord Jesus Christ – and that's for real!

We knew it was for real because men had not just threatened us, but really wanted to hit us or knife us – and every time, our King of Kings the Lord Jesus came through for us!

One time we were minding our own business in a little shopping center area late at night. I went into the grocery store to get some food while John <u>watched</u> the packs. The Lord Jesus had told me to stop dilly-dallying, as I was prone to do, in the nice warm store, so I moved along and zipped on out and sure enough there was trouble. As I came out the door, there was John in a lively conversation with a couple of town thugs, threatening him, as he confessed his faith in Christ. Was John ever glad to see me! It was about 9pm and these guys were really rabble-rousers and drunk or drugged, as they started to threaten John and tried to throw a few punches. In a flash, John rebuked them in the name of Jesus and so did I. Suddenly these violent men backed off and walked away. Screeching at the top of their voice as a parting shot, "You're going to hell for saying that." That was the demons talking through them, of course, and John could see the black spirits speaking right through them. We laughed (a bit nervously) and said, "Let's get out of here!" And so we did. Safe and sound in the rainy night with our Friend the Holy Spirit doing his special brand of Holy Ghost karate. Poor guys didn't know what hit them, when men like this tried to hit us, they came up against that invisible wall of God's presence, and they didn't know why their hands couldn't meet our face. It was unnerving – and I'm sure they were never the same.

Chapter 41
No Bull – Macho! A Test

Well you might think size matters to the Lord – but it doesn't. We went to a little church in Southern California one time – It was a Bible study in someone's home and we had already been accepted by the pastor and been able to give our testimony in the main church – but people often want to test you when you're new. Well my husband wandered outside after the Bible study with the man of the house – sharing his testimony with this farmer. The farmer took John into his bull pen to meet the Black Angus Bull he had and to do a little work outdoors that he needed to do.

Suddenly, the bull – also threatened by a newcomer – started to paw the ground with his sharp cloven hoofs. He has his head down and he looked real mad, John later told me. The farmer said to John, "If you're scared, I can stand in front of the bull, John, and he won't hurt me – if you want me to." John perceived a challenge and stood his ground. Then John put his hand out to the angry bull, open handed, and said, "Mr. Bull (he was being polite), I bring to your attention the name of Jesus." Much to the farmer's surprise, the bull bowed it's formerly raised head and dropped down on all fours. This amazed the farmer, as the submission to him would be two legs down in front but the back legs up – But for the name of Jesus, he dropped down to all fours.

Later, John and the farmer came back into the house, excitedly sharing what had happened, to the rest of us. The farmer had been a "child" of missionary parents, who went to China for years, and was convinced now, that John and I were for real – Thank you Jesus! And he later blessed us that evening with a little cash before we left because he was so impressed!

Chapter 42
DIVINE APPOINTMENTS! – MALACHI 3:16-18

We often had sweet fellowship, me and John – and it was our fellowship with Jesus and each other, that would draw other souls to us. We were Jesus' fisherman – searching out the right places and good spots for fish, and waiting on Jesus to bring us those hungry souls while we fed on his Heavenly Manna. It was no pretense – it was our Calling, it was real and Jesus was there. I fellowship alone now, but I know Jesus is there from years of fellowship Divine, with my husband, John. I know how to pray and get my own Manna – and worship the Lord Jesus – although it's been a struggle since I was used to constant companionship with a beloved mate of 28 years. We did go to church occasionally as Jesus led us, but we were already well schooled in the Word of God as taught by the Holy Spirit. And as every missionary knows – when you're out in the field – you have to learn to get your own Manna. So that's how we did it, and we were always talking about Jesus because he was our focus – and praying at night for his Divine protection, praying and interceding for the souls we met – and always praying for direction. So it was no wonder, we were told by perfect strangers at times, that our faces were shining with the glory of God. As it says, "If you eye (your focus) be single, your body <u>will</u> be full of light."

I taught John how to spell "friend" – "i" before "e" which he never could remember because he didn't get to finish high school because he was so sick – so I said to him, "A friend will 'fri' with you to the 'end'." And so we did – because our greatest friend is Jesus and he always gives us perseverance and fellowship in all circumstances, even unto sickness and death. Even in the end when people saw me and John on the bus, they thought we were newlyweds because we were so in love.

One time we were in Texas, heading towards Austin, and we paused at a park by the road. We met a young man who was attracted to our life. We prayed for him and he was filled with the Holy Spirit. He had gone through hard times with his marriage, and so the Lord Jesus gave him a love high. We talked with him for hours, with his eyes looking away as we got into the deeper things of God. We looked at each other knowingly – he was a baby Christian – and just like a real baby, when he doesn't understand you he starts looking above you and all around. So it is with a young Christian, we had observed many times. So we parted after a while, knowing he was well fed with the word of God, and headed on our way, and he headed south and we headed to San Marcos, Texas. That was a caught fish and we interceded for his soul afterwards – as he had been healed by Jesus of many wounds, he confessed. Jesus even gave him a healing of memories because he needed it.

Another time in Del Rio, Texas, a man of African American decent approached us by the beautiful Del Rio River. We had just had a lovely swim, until John saw a water snake following me – and I got out of that water fast. John was laughing and we watched the snake take some catch of fish down beneath his water hole in the stream – probably a water moccasin – Anyway, we were laughing and enjoying ourselves by the river and this man came over with a little extra food he had and shared it with us. He was traveling low-style like us – he was attracted to our light and cheer as well – and we fellowshipped in the Lord. Eventually he confessed how his adulterous wife had left him, and now she was living in his (her husband's) home with this guy. And he wanted to kill him. So he wisely took off on the freights – as he knew the Lord and asked us to pray for him not to go back and get revenge but to continue to travel. We did and he became joyful and we all said goodbye as he caught the freights further on. And that was another fish Jesus was watching over – he already knew the Lord Jesus, but Jesus wanted to keep him safe and sound from the enemy's terrible foils. Because my husband and I lived holy lives – we had built up an anointing from serving Jesus faithfully, and laying down our life for the brethren continually, so our prayers set the captives free – and then we'd go and intercede. I still live a holy life and I remain a celibate in my remaining years on earth, thus far, so I can set the captives free. After all, I lost the love of my life after 28 years of sweet heavenly success, and he is irreplaceable to me. Until further notice, I am biding my time down here solo.

When we traveled we never begged or panhandled – but we tried to keep the integrity of the spirit and not to look at people as dollar signs. We <u>occasionally</u> got food stamps, if the Lord Jesus told us to – but usually we just lived by faith – (except when John got sick the last 4 ½ years of his life and he was able to get on SSI – Because he was on dialysis and that is extremely costly, $500 a treatment, 3 times a week, we had to.) That's how we survived – <u>by faith</u> – for at least <u>23</u> years of our married life. Living by faith was very challenging and we never looked down on the panhandlers – but we just didn't feel called to do that... we wanted to see the Lord provide by being meek and patient. One time we met a brother in the faith who did pan-handle. He had back-slidden into alcoholism and was trying to overcome, but had a <u>very</u> interesting and provocative lesson from the Lord Jesus Christ. We met him at this Hispanic mission in Colton, California, where they fed the poor with a lovely Mexican dinner, every afternoon, on the patio of this church. We were there often, as Colton was a junction and regular meeting place for the freight train travelers, where you could head east to L.A., then Las Vegas, or west to Palm Springs and Arizona, eventually.

Anyway, we were chatting with a couple men at the mission feast and he was one of them. So this bearded man from Alaska, who noticed we were Christians, wanted to fellowship with us. We eventually became friendly and at the park, one day, he told us his testimony. He had studied in Alaska, at a Bible seminary to become a pastor. It was a group called "Abbot Luke". Ever since he was young it was prophesied that he would be a preacher – well he had some pride still in him, as we all do, and when he was in his apartment upstairs, in Alaska, he used to look at the bums on the street, pan-handling and drunken – and say to himself how despicable they were – how he'd <u>never</u> be like that. He was being a typical Pharisee without realizing it... In a sudden turn of events, he left Alaska, and went to Seattle and something happened to him. He started drinking and before he knew it he was out on the street living homeless, pan-handling for a drink, and eventually he got into riding the freight trains. It was a real "Nebuchadnezzar" Daniel ch.4, experience for him. He had traveled by freight all the way from Seattle to Colton, when we met him. It was evident through his testimony that the Lord was putting him through this abasement and teaching him a lesson or two. Well we camped out nearby and walked around a few days together, and he got real fired up and happy – as Jesus blessed him with more light and power through fellowship and our prayers of intercession for him. He told us that he had asked the Lord Jesus, if it was alright that he pan-handled, and the Lord Jesus told him that it was okay, but to be <u>honest</u> and not lie. So he always told the truth after that, and God blessed him in his humble pan-handling as he was overcoming his drinking habit. We were walking one day and he confessed that he had a fear of dogs, and we shared with him how we rebuked mean dogs and people in the name of Jesus. He hadn't experienced a lot of the power of God yet, so it just wasn't getting through to him. Suddenly, a little wiener dog came right at his heals yapping away – I was tempted to ignore it because of its size – but the Lord Jesus said to me, "He fears dogs and that dog will bite him if you don't do something." I thought of the scripture that says, what you fear shall come upon you, Job 3:25. So I turned and rebuked the dog at his heels, in the name of Jesus! And John and I were amazed because that little dog literally flew back – like a mighty force had pushed him. It usually wasn't quite so dramatic! But the Lord had it done for his sake! And then I said to this man, nonchalantly, "See it works." And he replied with great amazement, "I can see it does!"

So even though dogs don't <u>always</u> fly backwards when we rebuke them in the name of Jesus, though God does stop them every time – John and I could see this was a special demonstration of God's power at work – just to convince <u>this</u> believer, that the Holy Ghost was a powerful person to be reckoned with and could protect him from dogs or predatory demons in people – as we had shared with him.

And in conclusion, when we parted with this up and coming pan-handler for Jesus, he told us he truly had gotten edified because he saw by me and John's life and testimonies, on the road for years – that Jesus didn't have to put him in a church building with a pulpit like he imagined, to teach and minister the word of God, but he could use him right where he was at, on the road or riding as a freight train tramp and traversing the United States. Thus he was back on "track" and newly revolutionized in his thinking and departed with joy! And that was another story where Jesus had us fishing for a soul, who "lost his way", who knew Jesus, but just needed to be rejuvenated, and restored. And because our faces shown like wise men do, and we always talked about Jesus – those souls would come right up to us in the waters of life – that Jesus wanted to set free.

Malachi 3:16-18, "And they that fear the Lord, spoke often one to another – and the Lord harkened, and heard it, and a book of remembrance was written before Him, for them that feared the Lord and that thought upon His name.
And they shall be mine, saith the Lord of hosts, in that day when I make my jewels: and I will spare them, as a man spareth his own son that serveth him.
Then shall ye return, and discern between the righteous and wicked, between him that serveth God and him that serveth Him not."

Chapter 43

JAMES BOND/CONSPIRACY-TREACHERY

Psalm 82:5 "They know not, neither will they understand: they walk on in darkness: all the foundations of the earth are out of course."

Ah, if life was as simple as a James Bond movie – remember how James would have a hot date, maybe she'd give him a flower, and while she was in the bathroom he'd check it out and find a poison dart in it. He'd confront her, the date would end... Something like that. But I may have made that one up. But at any rate – the idea is that the treachery was discovered early by clever James Bond.

We all have to use our minds like James did to discover treachery – James was fictional, but I understand the writer, Ian Fleming, really had some real life experiences in the spy arena – he had this ingenious mind, but we in Christ though we can't be "paranoid" or overly suspicious of people, which would interfere with the love of Christ. We nonetheless have the mind of Christ as it says in 1 Corinthians 2:16. We must be, "wise as serpents, and harmless as doves," Matthew 10:16 – "Children of malice but men in understanding," 1 Corinthians 14:20 – And although we don't seek to save our life, or we will lose it (self-preservation), as it says in Matthew 16:25, but we must also seek to be watchful, and not throw our life away. It's a balancing act, and only the Holy Ghost inside of a True Believer, can execute such wise judgment. Some preachers will say "never judge" – But you do," judge righteous judgment," Jn.7:24. Even ol' James Bond searched out the clues, not because she was gorgeous – outward appearance, but because he happened to sense danger. We who are saved, have more than animal instincts at our disposal. We who are in Christ have Holy Ghost instincts. While

Jesus Himself said, "Judge not, that ye be not judged"Mt.7:1. And a few lines later he said, "Cast not your pearls before swine and give not that which is holy unto dogs, lest they turn and rend you." (Matthew 7:6) Obviously a judgment of the Spirit is activated here, for you must discern if someone is swine – and we've all met swine in our spiritual encounters. Jesus also said, "Before you take the splinter out of somebody else's eye, take the log out of your face. Then you might see a little clearer." (Matthew 7:4-5) Again, the statement is clear that we're allowed to judge, only as much as we have overcome, but if we haven't overcome that sin that we criticize somebody else for, we need to take the log out of our face, first.

One time in Hawaii, we were friends with a man – who seemed to enjoy our friendship as we were all homeless and camping on the beach for free where it was allowed. He came from California also and he had some Christian background. Eventually he seemed rather irritated by us, more and more, and grew morosely jealous of our oneness as a couple – as we were newlyweds and very much in love. He became very negative around us. One day he shared with us a romantic encounter he'd had that was a misadventure that God chastened him for. He shared that he was kissing around with a young woman, under a palm tree and a centipede landed right on his lip that fell from the tree. It painfully stung his lip, large and swollen. We all laughed at such a clear warning from the Lord!

A short while later when things were turning sour with our friendship – because of his jealousy – we had an encounter with a "critter." You can leave your tent on the beaches on the rainy side of Oahu and take off – usually – provided you don't have an "expensive" tent that is showy. So we'd leave our tent unattended, though zipped up with our stuff, and take the bus into town. Ours was a very common little mountain tent that, we could barely sit up in. Well, one night, we came back and slept until morning and I was adjusting my pillow of clothes and backpack, and what was lying under my homemade pillow, I suddenly saw, was a centipede! Laying quite still and in shock from being discovered. We quickly killed it and got rid of it – thankful we had caught it in time. As I rested, musing how the centipede got under my pillow with the tent zipped up, the Lord Jesus gave me a vision of this young man's face with the centipede. So then I knew that he had placed it in the tent, (as the Holy Ghost was showing me), to get even. So that put an end to that artful dodger – and we decided to distance ourselves after that and he pretty much disappeared on his own because he felt so guilty.

So that was one of my first encounters with obvious treachery. John had had many on the road before he met me in his seven years of hitchhiking. And obviously there was no awareness on our part or cleverness, but just pure Holy Spirit protection keeping me from slipping my hand under the pillow and getting stung in the night and screaming to high Heaven.

Now the Lord God is not always lovey-dovey with enemies. The Bible makes it clear in 2 Samuel 22:26-27, NIV, that "unto the pure I will show myself pure etc., and unto the devious I will show myself devious." I just read an example of this in the Bible in an account of Elisha the prophet. The enemy came to attack Elisha and his servant with horses and chariots and soldiers, hoping to take him back to the king of Syria who hates him and wants to kill him. But Elisha's eyes are open and he sees an angelic host on horses and chariots of fire protecting him. His servant is scared so Elisha prays that God opens up his eyes as the enemies are coming towards him. He also prays that God blinds these enemies. God does – he literally blinds them and they are all running into each other. Elisha calmly walks up to them in their blinded state and doesn't identify himself, but says, "The town you are seeking is over here. I'll lead you there." And he takes them right to Samaria, the stronghold of Israel, where the king is at, and then prays that God opens up their eyes. They are shocked. King Jehoram of Israel, says, "Should I kill them?" Elisha says, "No, feed them and send them home." So God has Elisha being devious through Him, though kind in the end to these enemies! 2 Kings 6:15-22

Sometimes God will have you use your mind to outwit your enemies, along with His supernatural intervention. As my husband would always pray – "have the Holy Ghost in us out-fox the foxes and predators today, in Jesus' name."

We had another encounter of treachery, also in Oahu where we camped 11 months, on the "Big Island", as well as Oahu, where it was free on the rainy side with a permit. We ran into this man who was the local drug dealer of the beach. He was high on drugs when we met him, and asked us if we were Jehovah's Witnesses or something. We said that we were born-again Christians! "Well," he said, "I knew you were something because I saw light all over you." So we had a rapport with him, though not exactly a friendship, as we were so different.

He would sometimes try to push his drugs on us when we were sharing food together at our table, thinking we'd at least smoke marijuana – but we'd always say no. It got annoying, his bugging us – so my husband prayed for an answer to his constant nagging, and the Lord told him a good one. So the next time this guy came by our table and he tried to persuade us again to get high, John said, "Listen, we're not trying to change your lifestyle so don't try to change ours." This man never forgot that! When the Holy Ghost gives you a Heavenly *rhema* word you never forget it – it's burned right into you. We never forced the gospel on this man and he knew it. He'd have to ask us and then we'd share a testimony with him because the Bible says in Revelation 22:11, "them that are filthy let them be filthy still..." And like William Penn, the Quaker, said "Force make hypocrites, persuasion makes converts."

Well, some months later I was alone with this little group that hung out with the local drug dealer they called the "Caveman". John was working at a labor pool job, so I was alone at the camp. They offered me a beer – well me and John knew the Bible teaches liberty to drink but in "temperance" – so we would occasionally have a glass of wine or beer, though we didn't have to have it. So I had a beer with these folks and I was offered another and I said no thanks, knowing my limits. One of the guys, who was a friend of the Caveman, spoke up. "Oh yes," he said in a mocking sneering voice, "that's right, the 'Christians' don't drink more than one beer!" And on and on he went, really getting mean about it. Out popped the Caveman, from his tent and said, "Listen man, she's not trying to change your lifestyle so don't change hers!" Wow! Incredible! Months later, yet! And amazingly, all the others said,

"Yes, yes, we know," as if they had heard it often. Well John and I later laughed at this, knowing how the Holy Spirit had made that word alive to him. God's word does not return void! Isaiah 55:11.

Towards the end of our stay – we felt the Lord Jesus had clearly told us to leave, and my husband even saw a large anointing of the Holy Spirit that it was time to leave. But because we owed a man John loved a debt, we wanted to pay it off. So we were trying to paint his father's boat. Well, this was in Honolulu, and every time we tried to paint the boat, it would rain. As soon as we'd get started on a bright sunny day, it would rain. We didn't have permission to stay on the boat overnight so we'd have to go back to the beaches on the other side of the Island. So even though John had seen a lot of light and anointing, to leave Hawaii after 9 months, and we even had the means – we stayed two months after that date trying to paint this boat for his friend. We paid for this bad decision. The Caveman was getting irritated by us Christians getting in the way of his possibilities – like beautiful young women interested in the gospel, just when he was hoping to seduce them into drugs, etc. As the sick "Caveman" joke was, we figured out, he would get them into his tent and hit them over the head with drugs and seduce them. So he got annoyed with us, and wanted to get rid of us, and sent a couple of his bad guys to get rid of us. We were rudely awakened one morning, as all of a sudden "something" was hitting our tent. We opened the door to find a bunch of Hawaiian guys throwing spears at us, the kind you use for spear-fishing with a long rubber band and then you let go and it hits the target. So meanwhile, John had jumped up from a dead sleep and a glass pickle jar broke as they threw these spears at us. John kneeled on it and I was shocked. It was my first year out in the field. John was bleeding and they were throwing their spears. So we rebuked them in the name of Jesus, but we didn't have a lot of power with them as we were supposed to have left two months before. Then we looked at this Japanese family picnicking nearby, who witnessed the whole thing, but they didn't want to help us either, as they were local Hawaiians and hated "haulis" or whites – which is quite prevalent in Hawaii. So we left our tent and these crazy guys, and John and I called the fireman from a nearby phone for his bleeding knee. They came quickly and took us to the nearby paramedic station and bandaged up his knee. He was a local Portugeuse-Hawaiian. The Paremedic said to us in a sarcastic voice, "You haulies should go back to where you came from!" And we did... And when we flew back to Seattle, WA., John kissed the ground he was so happy to be back.

And the moral of that story is, being in the right place at the right time helps in battles with treacherous souls. For then you have power over your enemies. When it's time to leave – don't be beholden to your friends. Just go! Because God knows all things, as we learned painfully. "When a man's ways please the Lord, He makes his enemies to be at peace with him." Proverbs 16:7. And He did, of course, until we ignored God's signal to leave. As the Bible says, "They think it strange you run not with them to the same excess of riot, speaking evil of you." 1 Peter 4:4

*hauli: means white pig – as there is no word in the Hawaiian language for white

Chapter 44

BATTLING THE STORMS IN WEATHER AND IN PEOPLE

Ephesians 6:10-18 – We fight not against flesh and blood but wicked spirits in high places…

Sometimes we were stuck in a town no matter how hard we tried to get out. We had left Grand Island, Nebraska, and even getting to the town of Hastings was a struggle. As we walked the 20 or so miles to Hastings, Nebraska, we paused by a creek and had our tent up and we were finishing a nice meal we had cooked for ourselves. The sky was dark and cloudy and it was late afternoon. As I rinsed my pan in the creek, la de da, taking my time, suddenly I heard the Lord speak to me clearly, and say – "Get inside the tent." At first I ignored the voice, continuing to wash the pan, but suddenly I thought, "That was the Lord! I better listen." So I headed into the tent with John, and as soon as we got into the tent, a strong wind came out of nowhere – and we were smitten. Our little tent was actually flattened to the ground with us in it. The fiberglass poles of the tent bending as low as I'd ever seen – the wind was whistling and suddenly I felt like Dorothy in the tornado! It was a mighty wind! We cried out to the Lord to save us – rebuked the wind – we did it all! We cried out to the Lord from our tent, that it wouldn't be whipped away from us. If John and I had not listened to the Lord on time, our tent would have been floating down the river without us to anchor it down. Finally, after what seemed like forever – the winds died down more moderately, so that our poles weren't bending in half violently, and we made it through the night. (I have since learned from other transients often the poles do snap in such storms! Praise God!)

Hastings was a sight the next day when we walked into it, and we thanked the Lord Jesus for saving us from the entire rocket of stuff flying around, and that we didn't take off, <u>or</u> our tent. It wasn't called a tornado – but it was considered one heck of a wind storm. Quite a bit of debris was all around.

We didn't expect to stay in Hastings – I think we were rather nervous after that, and really didn't know the town – but as we sat there quietly by the railroad tracks – waiting about 4 hours for any train to stop – none did it seemed. We finally got up and asked the brakeman if any trains came by? He told us one had an hour ago, and it had paused. We realized we must have been blinded by the Lord, and he wanted us in town.

And it was so – he used us in a Pentecostal church – where we were asked to preach and later in a Methodist church where we stayed with the minister and his wife and children – and they even asked us through word of mouth to teach to a teenage group in a Lutheran church. Anyway, we had a great time and we were glad we obeyed, seeing the Lord Jesus Christ in all things. Although we did get much persecution in this town that was modestly small – and we became known as "those two" – As we stuck out like a sore thumb in this conservative little town – John with his somewhat long hair and us with our backpacks!

Hastings... the rest of the story...

Ah, Hastings – yes, it's been quite a while but now I remember. That's where we met the Methodists who were blinded to us, much like the blinding testimony I mentioned earlier – and in fact, when we were at the railroad tracks trying to catch a train out – we'd already had some fireworks, and that's why we were exiting out of town. In fact, we met a pleasant man at a coffee place – like McDonalds – and he was an assistant pastor and invited us to his house and we met his family. We were fairly well received as they were Pentecostal, and we were charismatic as well. They even asked us both to preach because of the Holy Ghost witness on our testimonies that they heard. Well, whenever you're hot for Jesus, you <u>are</u> <u>controversial</u>! So we found out how hot we were! Especially John!

I preached on Philippians 2:15-16 – about how we are to shine as stars forever, holding out the word of life to a corrupt generation (NIV) – and the difference between condescending to men in all things, and being condescending in a belittling way (Romans 12:16). John, on the other hand, preached on the famous apostolic chapter (1 Corinthians 4:11-13) NIV, as we knew we were "apostles" and this was a Pentecostal church, after all, that recognized apostle-prophets and the five-fold ministry. Apostle is just the more biblical word for missionary – and it means "sent one" in fact. But John dear, preached in 1 Corinthians 11 on what Paul says, that the apostles were homeless and despised and the scum of the earth – <u>not men in three-piece suits</u>! He did a wonderful job, as John was very non-pretentious and a bold speaker. He unknowingly had pushed some buttons, though, as they had an apostle leader who was away and he dressed in a three-piece suit and was given much authority over this church. Afterwards, different people complimented both of us on our preaching and even some told John they felt the anointing – a good witness on our testimonies – but there seemed to be some hidden controversy, as we later found out. So we got back to this young man Lyle's home, who had brought us to his church, and we learned the scoop that there was an apostle over the whole church who was on a journey at present, and he was a hot-shot who wore three-piece suits, or something like that, and John stepped on some toes, as he had emphasized that apostles were people that were very persecuted, and as Paul the Apostle said, were considered the scum of the earth.

That evening we tried to relax in this young couple's home. They ushered us into the TV room where they had on a glitzy TBN couple, who were still an item before their abasement. Well, John and I suffered a lot on the road and weren't easily taken in by the glamour queens of TBN who begged for money. So we tried to watch it a little, and as the wife was crying the blues for this and that, and John got up and I agreed, so we moved away from the TV. The couple were surprised as they observed us from the kitchen, and said, "What's wrong?!" John stated without guile, "We're not into that candy and ice cream gospel!" Well they were! And they bantered with us for a bit on the subject to no avail. And we parted the next morning, I believe. So, it was a moment of glory – a moment was all it was.

Soon thereafter, we went to a Bible study that we had been invited to by some Methodists – a women named Virginia and the assistant pastor's wife named Valera. Valera invited us to her home after the study, but at first we were so discouraged by our first experience in Hastings, we headed out to the railroad tracks instead. I think even Virginia asked us over, too. Anyway, we tried to escape and God blinded us to the railroad trains, as I already expressed – as he had done on another occasion with a local bus when we were supposed to stay put. So after our failed attempt to leave, John admitted he felt led to go visit the Methodist people who had received us well already – better than the Pentecostal people did! – As we got solace with them and some fellowship that lasted.

God had to blind some "people" to us in this town as well, because there was quite a little lynch mob when the "big apostle" of the Pentecostal church came back. His little gang wanted to do us in, and John would literally see the Holy Spirit blinding them to us – because we dared to come against that so-called "great apostle" – they were stalking us. Whatever their reasons, they were not good, for God supernaturally protected us a number of times.

Next, we were asked to speak in a Lutheran compass church, as well – to some teenagers, via this Methodist church that had some charismatic leaders so could recognize the gifts of God in our lives. Our stay, which lasted about a month, turned out to be quite eventful and fruitful.

Ironically, we passed through there a year or so later, and found out that the Pentecostal church that had given us a hard time, had gone defunct and was no more.

"Many are the afflictions of the righteous: but the LORD delivers him out of them all!" Psalm 34:19.

And as I shared earlier, Valera and Jerry's boy, Andy, had been blinded to us when he went looking for us. And even Valera, when she came by in her car, couldn't see us either, when she wanted to give us a ride, right after we left their home for a walk. As I said, God wanted to show them that the blinding power of God was real, that we had testified to, as well, in our many travels.

Chapter 45

Gino: Eyes of Death

One time John and I were riding the freight trains through the mountains of California, heading towards Nevada and eventually Utah. The train paused in the mountains somewhere still in California and it was all desolate forest. It was a windy mountain road and the engineer had to wait for another train to pass. It was one of those long waits so we hopped out of our little grain car. We could tell it was stopping for a while because they let the air out of the brakes... *chchchchoooo*! That was the sound. John and I had some coffee on us and a can to cook with so we made a little coffee by the side of the road – making a little fire and heating up the water, and throwing in the coffee grounds, brown sugar, and evaporated milk.

As we relaxed, along came three guys, walking from the freight train, looking at us with keen interest. It's always unusual to see a woman (me) on the tracks so I'd come to expect that reaction. So we got to talking – and of course we shared our faith in Christ. The guy that seemed like the ring-leader, I couldn't help but notice his eyes were like pits and I remember thinking it was like I could see death or hell in them. Then, shortly after, he told us how he spent 20 years in prison for <u>murder</u> and when he got out recently, he just wanted to ride the freight trains and be free! We understood that all right! As we shared with this man, Gino, and his friends, how we would rebuke men in the name of Jesus to protect ourselves – he suddenly pulled out a switchblade and started flipping it around, playing with it in a very menacing way – with that murderous look in his eyes. We knew it was the old game – you show me your weapon (rebuking people in the name of Jesus) – now I'll <u>show</u> you mine. It's really the demons in the person that was threatened by our testimonies of spiritual warfare – "for we wrestle not against flesh and blood- but against spiritual wickedness in high places." (Ephesians 6:11-12) Gino's weapons were carnal, but his demons were doing their best to terrorize us. Well, thank God the air was put back in the brakes again, so we all meandered back to our grain cars, knowing it would take off soon enough – which it did. The three guys had been riding about ten grain cars behind us, where their stuff was, and so they returned there.

Well it was a long night, the train slowly wound around the mountains going through California then Nevada. These men had been at least ten grain cars behind us, like I said, and we noticed a strange thing – whenever the train would pause, for whatever reason, they would jump off and move up closer to us – then next stop closer yet. Slowly they were making their way up, grain car by grain car, towards us, every time it paused, though there was no reason to do so. I felt literally unglued and quite upset and my asthma even acted up, that the Lord Jesus had <u>not</u> yet healed. John comforted me, but I could tell he was deeply disturbed too – as we were traveling through desolate places and he always cherished me as his great love, so we prayed a whole lot. This was a mile and a half long train and we were nearer to the back than the front. Finally the train stopped in a little town, around late morning, in Nevada. It was the "junction" town where the train always stopped and where they would switch cars around – take off stuff or add it. So we relaxed. At least it was daylight now – But we were still looking at another overnight ride to make it to Ogden, Utah.

So we got off our grain car, seeing in the daylight that sure enough these guys were moving their way up, and they were just three cars behind us now, instead of ten. As we stood by our car, though, along came a car-knocker* guy, named Fred, looking concerned. "Hey," he said, "those guys look like they're up to no good – why don't you come with me for lunch at my house, and get away for awhile." We looking knowingly at each other, thinking Fred must have heard them say something <u>pretty</u> <u>bad</u>. "You can have lunch with us, me and my wife." Well, we knew Fred was a Godsend and we hopped into his truck merrily and chatted as he drove through the small desert town to his home.

We told him he was a Godsend and Fred amazingly turned to us and said, "I am an <u>atheist</u>, but something told me to help you out." He was 70 years old, but his hair was still dark and it wasn't even dyed. He told us how he had known to pick us up as he sensed danger and had worked the railroad all his life. He told us his wife was a born-again Christian though, and would enjoy meeting us. We got there and his much younger wife, about in her 40's, fixed us a great meal and we had great fellowship with them all – sharing our testimonies. She was interested that we were born-again like her and Fred even liked hearing our adventures because they were on the railroad tracks, like his job. So it was a peaceful, lovely time.

Around early evening Fred took us back, when it was starting to get dark. He said he was going to move us a bit, and he brought us in his truck way up to the front, in this mile and a half long train, knowing the train would be leaving in minutes. Fred got us into a nice boxcar, this time, and we were quite comforted, knowing even when the train went around the bends; we couldn't be sighted by those evil men. We arrived in Ogden, Utah – early morning – and we watched with delight as we got off the boxcars and crossed over a wide bunch of tracks. And we saw those guys way down at the other end, in the dim light of early morning (about 5am), also crossing the tracks and pointing at us out with shock, wondering how we ever got way up there, without them seeing us! We laughed and praised the Lord Jesus Christ! And we thanked Him for his unusual messenger – saved by an atheist as directed by the living God. God bless Fred!–Which means peace – he sure brought us peace.

John, my husband, who was of course thrilled too, because he wasn't a natural pacifist – coming from Pittsburgh, Pennsylvania from a family of steel mill workers – which he probably would have been one too, if he hadn't been so sick with ulcerative colitis, since 8 years old. Of course God had other plans! John always said to me that if anyone tried to hurt me, he'd want to kill them and he even added that if God didn't come though, he would! But we yielded to our spiritual weapons always! And God always came through somehow, as our Lord Jesus Christ is an "ever present help in times of trouble."

*car knocker (Fred's occupation) – railroad worker in charge of rolling the new pieces into the connecting train so that the cup-links knock together and interlock.

～

By the way, God used another atheist in Capitola, California, near Santa Cruz, I can't help but remember. We were sitting next to a candy factory and very famished from walking with our big backpacks. So we checked the candy factory dumpster for throw away candy, after all candy is great energy food. A man walked up to us, who had observed us – and he handed us a box of peanut brittle (he worked there) and a five dollar bill. We thanked him profusely and praised the Lord Jesus because we had run out of money completely. He smiled amazingly, and said, "I'm an atheist, but something told me to give you this five dollar bill!" Ha ha! I guess God was making a believer out of him, as he did likewise with dear Fred.

Chapter 46

ON WOMEN – BODY LANGUAGE

John was a "sweetheart" in general, and a champion for women. He treated me as his equal and so I became his equal. What I mean is, he could have lorded over me with his 14 ½ years older than my age, or his 8 older years in Christ as a sold-out Christian. John knew "body language" and learned it diligently as a hobby – he read a famous book called "Man Watching" by Desmond Morris, an anthropologist. He would show me men's macho body language when they weren't receiving what I was saying. Like, if you put your hands crossed behind your head, that can mean superiority – like in a job interview, sometimes the boss will stick his feet up on the desk (very rude – feet in your face) and his hands crossed behind his head and say to the potential employee, "Tell me about yourself." Immediately they feel belittled – and that is the idea. It's a power trip!

So I'd be in someone's home, meeting new Christian people, and we'd be talking to some guys about the Lord Jesus. These men were talking about "fasting" to us. John could share freely, but when I stepped in to put my two cents in about fasting, they instantly did the superiority gesture. Well, in body language, if you want to break the negative message, you mirror it. So this time I was really fed up with men doing this gesture to me, and Christians yet, so when they did this to me, as I shared my "fasting experience" that I had gone through, immediately the guy I was facing put his arms above his head crisscrossed! Well, I did it back, and immediately he dropped his arms, sure enough, totally unaware of why he did it and why he stopped, as it was all unconscious usually. I finished my story competently, and John was laughing at the scenario. I had dropped my arms immediately when they did, as

I just wanted to be equal. Later he told these guys, if I recall correctly, what had happened so that they would be more self-aware. Often John would call men on their body language.

Another thing John taught me was how macho men would sometimes use Bible scriptures against women in a legalistic way. For instance, "women can't teach" was at times spoken harshly to me by a man when I was sharing some revelation the Lord Jesus gave me. Well John would say his famous line to that man, which he had learned in many battles, "The <u>Holy Ghost</u> is <u>not</u> retarded in <u>women</u> or <u>children</u>," and that would leave them flabbergasted.

We read a great book years ago called "Women in the Church" by Russell C. Prohl, and he said a lot of statements in the Bible about women in the church are in the context of a historical situation, such as the women at Corinth were of a heathen, unlearned background and previously were prophetesses for their false gods. So he was admonishing them to submit to learning the word of God first, and not teach. Obviously, Priscilla in the book of Acts, whose name is mentioned before her husband Aquila's name a couple of times, was learned and <u>taught</u> Apollos the word of God (Acts 18:18-28, Ro.16:3-4). So it helps to know the history and rightly divide the word of God, as we are told we are "neither male nor female in the church, but we are all one in Christ." (Galatians 3:27-28, Acts 2:17)

The other "killer" that macho men use against women is that women should be "silent in the church." Again, this is described in Russel C. Prohl's book as a cultural difference. In the sanctuaries back then, the Jewish women sat on one side while the men sat across on the other side – and they would call out to their husbands excitedly during the teaching of the word – to make comments – it sounded like a very "free-spirited" early church. So Paul was saying for women to be silent during the teaching, not to interrupt, and talk it over at home with their husbands – obviously there <u>were</u> female for instance Philip's the Evangelist's, four virgin daughters who prophesied who must have spoken in the church, as was mentioned in the Bible. Acts 21:8-9

I always remember meeting this guy who belonged to a "snake-handling" Pentecostal church where they actually pick up snakes to demonstrate their faith, and yes, people <u>do</u> get bit, he admitted. Well, he thought he was back-slidden because he left this church and it was very controlling, but we told him that was cultish and indeed leaving a church was his choice as long as he still loved Jesus and wanted to obey His will. He seemed relieved, as they had been very legalistic to him. Then I shared something I knew about the Lord Jesus to this man, and he suddenly said to me, "Women can't teach!" John and I looked at each other with disgust! My husband, John, said his famous line that Jesus had taught him in many battles with misogynist men – "The Holy Ghost is <u>not</u> retarded in women or children!" John was a real "champion of women" – so I continued a bit haltingly, and after a while the man forgets himself when I tell him something I learned through experience, and he says without thinking, "I never knew that!" And I said, "See, I taught you something!" (duh, right!) God wants Christians to use their minds and not just lash out with the word of God without comprehending it, or rightly dividing it – like the scriptures say, "the letter killeth but the Spirit giveth life," 2 Cor. 3:6. We are, after all, neither male nor female in the oneness of Christ. We are all adopted <u>sons</u> of God, equal inheritors of the gospel. (Romans 8:4-6,, John 1:12)

On children, although they may lack maturity – but we all do when we are born again – we all start as babes – Of course life experiences help, <u>nonetheless</u>, a child has an edge if he or she is really on fire for Jesus – "Child-like faith" – Jesus said, we have to come as "children" to enter the kingdom of God and have child-like faith, Matt.18:2-4. Some people think "intelligence is goodness" – and put their <u>brains</u> on a pedestal, as I saw in a vision– but intelligence can lead you to evil – malevolent evil – <u>as well as</u> to goodness – and the Christian must train him or herself to trust in God and pray for divine intelligence, and that takes child-like faith and being born again, trusting the living God!

John and I read a great book in the 70s or 80s called <u>Like a Mighty Wind</u>, by Mel Tari. This was about a Micronesian group who got converted to Jesus. They didn't have a lot of Americana knowledge and technological escapism and they took the word of God completely by faith – as a result, when they went forth to preach the word in the jungles of Micronesia, they had amazing experiences of walking on water, healing the sick, raising the dead, and even were severely poisoned by a cannibal tribe and lived to tell about it and see the tribe converted. The tribe converted because they had given them enough poison to kill a rhinoceros. Also, the children of these missionaries who went with their parents had amazing colorful visions, like TV, and Jesus would speak to them and help the whole group out. So there is child-like faith through children and adults!

John noticed women had more sensitivity in certain areas than men. A woman may think more through her heart – as the heart sometimes can discern trouble sooner or discern better – <u>if</u> the woman is pure in her heart with the Lord Jesus. Several pastors that John met, actually would <u>use</u> their wives to discern a new person they met. Whereas a man may be more logical to overlook certain things, which is helpful at times, like quick decision-making, for instance, but can also cause them <u>not</u> to discern certain emotional needs or signs of trouble. So one hand helps the other.

I'm so glad that for the 28 years that I knew John and was able to enjoy his love, that he had the "champion of women" certificate from Jesus – and he still has one up in Heaven – as I saw a vision of him recently, writing a scroll up in Heaven with blue-silver anointing light of the Holy Spirit all over him, and the subject was "women". So that's why I knew to write this chapter!

And Jesus is our greatest "champion of women" – as you noticed He always edified women who were treated as second rate in Jewish society. Like the woman at the well who was shocked He asked her as a Samaritan John 4:7-29, <u>and</u> a women yet, for a cup of water – which moves me to share an interesting story about a minister we met who had a problem with women.

The minister wasn't always a misogynist but he got in with some Mormon influences that were very sexist and one-sided about women. They had infiltrated his Pentecostal church, sidling up to him and subtly influencing this pastor, creating something of a macho monster in him, as well. This was, after all, home of the Mormon teachings, the capital Salt Lake City of Utah, where the big Latter Day Saints sanctuary is, that sits on the city center, complete with a spike on top (no cross).

We met this Pentecostal man in our travels, who was attracted to us, as he and his wife had done street preaching on occasion, before their pastorship in Utah. This is why we said he <u>changed</u>, because when they were young, he and his wife did street evangelism as equals and they were quite a team. And he treated her as an equal, not beneath him as a second class citizen.

In the early century, the great Theologian Tertullian, who admired Christians and eventually took on a lot of their beliefs, as he observed them in his keen studies. He was amazed to see that in no other religion, except Christianity, are the men and women treated as equals in a marriage. In other religions, a woman is subservient to the man, but only in Christiandom, he observed "together they prayed, together they fasted, together they ministered." This is how it should be and it makes for a great team working for God's kingdom. Now the macho spirit where one is superior to the other has permeated many Christian factions as well, <u>not</u> just Mormons – but it is not the Lord! It is really just men insecure with their own power!

When a man is "secure" he shares the power with his wife and doesn't hoard it, thus creating perfect harmony and balance that is oneness. You can't have oneness with one-upmanship! As my husband often said, a man may be the head of his wife – but she is second in command as a first mate to a captain – <u>not</u> as a deckhand like a lot of men treat their wives. A first mate on the ship knows <u>all</u> the captain knows, and can take over the ship as needed, <u>any time</u>. It is just a matter of order that one of the two of them has a God-given ability to give the decisive edge to matters, thus diffusing arguments. But the first mate can challenge the captain and help him in difficult matters and decisions, and it was really a mutual business – otherwise they wouldn't be "one", duh!

Anyhow, this lovely couple who were hospitable to us for a few weeks, really had a great congregation and great worship, and we learned from some of their positive experiences in the Lord – But again, we were prophets and God would often give us the edge of seeing the fly in the ointment – it was our job. This pastor had gotten caught up in the mainstream religious thinking against women that permeated the town as well. So much so that he even refused to take his beautiful wife on a mission trip to India, even though their children were grown. Later he admitted, though he was greatly used of God with signs and wonders, he had truly needed his other half there. She was so grieved at being left behind, she became deathly ill at home by herself, but God blessed her too, with visions. He also had been belittling her about finances, all of which she was <u>entirely</u> aware of, although he <u>acted</u> like she was stupid.

One night while John was having a restless sleep in the little room, they let us sleep in, he actually semi-awoke and spoke out loud as clear as can be, "We burn our bridges behind us – we burn our bridges behind us." I asked him in the morning if he heard himself say that. And he didn't remember it and was quite surprised that he had said that in his sleep. Wondering about this mysterious nightly message, we got up the next morning and decided to eat breakfast with them. During breakfast they were observing their little grandson who was about 4 and very stalky and had this bad habit of pushing a little girl cousin down to the ground. She fell right down to the ground and they all laughed, but John and I felt grieved. One person commented, "That little boy loves to push little girls to the ground." Without thinking, my husband said, "Just like you," as he looked at the pastor. The pastor flushed red, all the way to the top of his head. My husband then cleared the air and spoke candidly, "Say man, do you consider women to be third class citizens?" "No," he answered, "I consider them to be second-class citizens!" At that, my husband and I stood up and told them that we had to leave now – and there was no argument as we gathered our stuff and said our goodbyes and thank yous' and went out the door! "We burn our bridges behind us!" And that was the end of that! We later wrote this man more of our thoughts on this matter, and we hoped he changed for the better – for one of our major functions in our ministry was "Balance." And this was the area he was off-balance in at the time, though greatly blessed in other areas – But "A false balance is an abomination to the Lord," Proverb 11:1 – and must be corrected! As the Holy Ghost is not retarded in <u>women</u> or <u>children</u>!!!

So that was the story on women! And how God wants to use them as much as men. In fact, during the Call for missionaries in China many years ago, for the first time – no men came forward but only women for the Chinese inland mission. Therefore they had women there as pastors, evangelists, apostles, to get this church started. Then they eventually trained men (of this country) – because it <u>was</u> a patriarchal society, to take over the new churches. But God is not sexist – he is looking for one thing – a willing heart! Amen!

Chapter 47

GREY GHOST

There's a train that goes so fast that the hobos call it the Grey Ghost. Some people guess it goes about 90 miles per hour. It's a mail train and it's all gray containers called piggy-backs! Some years ago we caught this train on several occasions, but it was always amazing how fast you got to where you were going – from El Paso to San Antonio, for instance – faster than we ever got there before by car or train. We had to be discreet riding this train – as they really preferred no riders – with such important cargo. Sometimes freight trains can be notoriously slow – especially if there is curvy terrain, like in the mountains, but not the "grey ghost". Well we enjoyed the "express" for a change when we could be so privileged to be there on time to catch it! It was breathtaking!

Now this is not a nice, safe boxcar we were in. It's a flat-car with a truck "trailer" on top. The trailer wheels are chained down and we would ride on the flat car between the two huge tires for a wind break. Quite exciting at 90 miles an hour… Jesus gave us faith to travel that way so that we could find those little lost lambs and sheep, and back-slidden shepherds that needed some heavenly wisdom, prayer, or fellowship, or deliverance along the way. It was torture sometimes with the wind-chill factor, but quite worth it when we met that gem of God's that had gotten dirty from the worldly trials and temptations.

Chapter 48

On Fire

One time John told me of an encounter he had on a city bus in his own travels by himself. Usually when John told me a testimony I would need to know it later on. He shared how a gay man sat next to him on the bus, and as the bus was moving along he started sidling his leg closer and closer to John until it was touching. John said in his prayer to the Lord Jesus and Holy Spirit, "If you don't stop him, Holy Spirit, I will" – and suddenly the man let out a yelp and said, "Oh, your leg is burning me up," and moved into his own corner.

I had a similar encounter with men on a freight train. These two guys purposely jumped from one grain car to our grain car, crossing over the cup-links as it was moving slowly, for no apparent reason, except that they hoped to encroach on me and overpower John. They did this when the train was moving slowly, and in polite hobo society you just don't do that! That may make you laugh, but even when hobos (or tramps) first meet each other they stand quite a distance away to prove that they were no threat – like 20 feet away – until more trust is formed. The idea is that no one intends to pull out a weapon, and that's how you show it with your body language – through distance. Anyway, these guys lingered on our little grain car shelf, very leeringly looking at us, especially me, and pretty drunk! The train was cruising and I was binding up their demons, and I'm sure John was praying too. I suddenly remembered John's testimonies about fire and I asked the Lord Jesus (in prayer), to bring fire down on them. What a reaction! Suddenly they hopped right over the cup-link while the train was moving pretty fast, to the next grain car – looking at us menacingly as if we had said something to them. They stayed away from us after that, for the rest of the ride! Ha ha!

Chapter 49

KLAMATH FALLS – JERRY ENCOUNTER

One time in Klamath Falls, Oregon, we had the thrill to ride a piggy-back without the truck-trailers on it – as they had already been delivered. Then the trucks come to pick them up. So what we had was a flat-car with some railings on it, which are where the trailer usually slides into. When the ride gets bumpy, you <u>hold</u> onto the rails for dear life, because you could bounce off. We were with a fellow tramp friend who we encountered from time to time. He had the blues and cared nothing for his life and was quite intoxicated – he fell asleep. Jerry was dangerously bouncing and passed out. He was a very <u>large</u> man and heavy – but with the rough road riding right through the mountains from Klamath Falls to California, he would have rolled right off, as there was no load to keep the ride steady. It was stressful to say the least, so John had me get on the other side of him to wedge him in so we could each hold on to him while he was passed out snoring. We held an arm on each side and were his human angels of mercy, until he made it onto steady ground, by Redding, California, and then we all made it to Roseville, CA and got off. He didn't even know he nearly died (although we let him <u>know</u> before he parted). We prayed for him, too, and I know the Lord's mercy was there for him on that ride. We parted our ways, our friend well rested now – and us a bit wired and tired, heading into Roseville Library to rest from our hair-raising, cold ride with a man who cared nothing for his life – but God sure did!

Chapter 50

MY "ORIGINAL" HUSBAND

John was an Original. He was very unique in his delivery of the gospel – and his personality was uniquely formed in Christ. One time, John told me, when he was traveling alone, a visiting prophet evangelist laid hands on him and said, by the Spirit, "you are an "<u>original</u>", a personality-plus", and he addressed how uniquely God was using him, and that he would suffer much persecution. Every evangelist that laid hands on him told him that, when he was beginning his ministry, and even just before he went on the road for Jesus – that he would have a unique and versatile ministry, that he would travel any way God intended him to and suffer great hardship for Jesus with persecution, and he should stick with it because God would really bless him. Which indeed he did, right up to the very end. Even when he was 12 years old and stood up to get saved, at a Katherine Kuhlman service, and got knocked down by the power of God (his Catholic relatives were astounded when he spoke in tongues for the first time). Then he was prophesied over by Katherine Kuhlman that he would travel for Jesus uniquely, any way that God wanted him to and would be a great "witness" for Jesus! It was amazing how he lasted for so long with an ileostomy from 24 years old, (no large intestine), and all the way to 66 years old... That is a long time to have an ileostomy, and I believe he maintained excellent health for years because of his faithfulness to Jesus. His health only failed him when we cared too much for treacherous fickle souls and laid down our lives for them – literally in John's case. John paid the price with his final years of being slandered and lied against in the occult factions, with devastating results, and in one case was even poisoned when we ended our fast too early. He suffered three strokes during that time, but God miraculously healed him and he lived another 12 years. I know he got many crowns up in Heaven for his 38 years of faithful service to King Jesus – as God even told me he was a "champion" and most men wouldn't have lasted as long or traveled low-style with an ileostomy. Well, we serve a worthy Savior, and our Calling together for 28 years was "blessed and fruitful" in a way that is unbelievable, and yet true!

A martyr's crown was the last crown he received and in his death he was given the victory through Christ Jesus. But we have power to live in Christ until God ordains for us to go, and then what's going to happen will happen. And so it goes even with a martyr's crown. As they tried to kill the apostles Peter and Paul at different times, but it didn't happen until Jesus let it happen. And I know Jesus saved John's life thousands of times and my life about seven hundred times at least, and I was so privileged to travel with a seasoned servant of the Lord Jesus, and become myself, a seasoned workman in God's field through my beautiful husband's experienced example and his cherished love for me. Many women thought I had it rough in the bourgeois sense, in not having the dream house or middle-class life, like the way I grew up as a child, but I was blessed with a dream husband with great tenderness that I often didn't see in those dream houses I met. My life went by like a beautiful dream-boat on a river, of endless testimonies, with the wind of the Holy Ghost moving us along. Our life experiences on the road were a string of pearls with divine togetherness, giving me "treasure" of priceless value – testimonies of high adventure – risking our necks for Jesus – we paid the price of a sold-out life – and it was breathtaking!!! With much tribulation you <u>will</u> enter the Kingdom of Heaven. Acts 14:22

I can still remember me, walking by John with his backpack, and then falling a bit behind him in tiredness, and he began talking, saying something to me, thinking I was still by his side. In a flash I'd get over to his <u>other</u> side to hear him, and he'd say, "Where you at?" and laughing, "Wow, you're fast!" I laughed too because no one ever called <u>me</u> fast. I was, because I loved him and still do in the heavenlies. He never lost his mystery to me – it was a divine romance – one given from Heaven – two focused on God, makes a perfect union that the Lord

Jesus sponsored and evolved for 28 years of wedded bliss… I'd do it all over again, and again, and again!

And so I will carry my cross, onward Christian soldier, as the Lord Jesus leads me, uniquely blessed by my buddy John's special anointing and refreshing love and sustaining gifts and always loving the "real me", like Jesus in him would do. He was a man I felt safe under the stars with, in his loving arms, in extreme vulnerability and exposure – more safe than mansions or riches or earthly havens, because God was truly his refuge and inspiration in all he did, with great abandon in awesome faith and a sweet, kind personality. Jesus says, "When I come back will I find faith?" I'm so glad I got a great arsenal of faith, legacy, and inheritance for myself to share with others to build their faith up. So I will carry on in faith as, "deep calls to deep", I look forward to sweet Jesus bringing me back to my husband John in glory land. There are other testimonies, but that is all I'm sharing for now. This string of pearls, an overview of our life, together as tramps for Jesus – as I know I have about 20 books in me to go, Lord willing!

I am now nearly seven years a widow and I continue to abide in His Life, the Lord Jesus, waiting with baited breath for all He has in store for me and His Kingdom, and the souls that await His call that I will encounter for Christ to be formed in them. With the Holy Spirit's love and Father's love, and the Lord Jesus' love, I go. I wait in my tent, <u>intent</u> on knowing Him better. Psalm 62

The End
Warrior

WARRIORS

"Thou wilt keep him(her) in perfect peace, whose mind is stayed on Thee: because he(she) trusteth in Thee. Trust ye in the Lord forever: for in the Lord JEHOVAH is everlasting strength."

Isaiah 26:3+4

Acknowledgements

Special Acknowledgments to: The Lord Jesus Christ, Father in Heaven, & Holy Spirit for leading me/us on these great adventures I always desired, plus giving us testimonies! And God & His Angels, for protecting me & my beloved, numerous times! As well as by myself! Thanks to:

Beloved husband John Ariel Gregory, whose faithful walk & special anointing, I could sync into! Such faith! (Already 7 years on the road.) For people that helped me get this book out, at the shelter of Santa Barbara, Ken Williams, who referred me to Coach Dave, who led me to Wendy Wright, when they heard I had written a book in my tent. Wendy thanks for hours on the computer, getting my book on a PDF. And Brian and Nancy Thibeault, for helping me get the book out with their home computer & tech knowledge & sending it. And for Nancy's dear mother, Marge, for encouraging me to try again to publish it, after she read the book. Thanks to Pastors Doug & Sandy Miller, for allowing me to be in a trailer etc., on their land, for almost 5 years! Thanks to all, for their loving care!!!

Printed in the USA
CPSIA information can be obtained
at www.ICGtesting.com
JSHW011505270124
56033JS00011B/275